Bound by Blood

My journey from the Mob to the Master

by Edmundo Ramirez
with
Ken Wade

All events portrayed in this work are based on the memory of the author, Edmundo Ramirez. Some details have been changed, and some names have been substituted.

DEDICATION

I want to dedicate this book to my brother Manuel for always being a great role model and to my brother Herman for teaching me how to be tough. Herman you were the forge and the fire. Manuel you were the hammer and the anvil. Together you shaped a man.

And to my sister Katy for all the times you patched up my wounds and all the packages and support while I was in the pen. You always believed in me even in my darkest hours.

I thank you all.

ACKNOWLEDGMENTS

First of all I want to acknowledge my spiritual parents, Pastor Augie and Mary Barajas. Thank you. Without you I couldn't have made it this far.

Pete and Nellie Ruiz, you never feared the darkness. You reached in and pulled the treasure out.

Vanessa, Eli, and Jeremy Barajas, you released your parents to work with men like me. Thank you for your sacrifice.

Evangelist Julio Alas, thank you for giving me the idea of writing this book and praying it into existence.

Sharon Cervantes, thank you for all your hours of hard labor in writing the skeleton that led to this book.

Thank you to my wife and three beautiful daughters for your unconditional love.

Thank you Pastor Sonny and Julie Arguinzoni for surrendering your lives to answer the call to reach Treasures out of Darkness. I am one of them.

My Lord and Savior Jesus Christ who covers me in his blood. To You I am bound by blood, Your blood.

CONTENTS

Chapter 1

I stood in the doorway looking in. Alone, immobile, unable to move forward or turn and run.

The rhythm of drums and bass guitar washed over me. A hundred voices sang while two-hundred hands clapped to the beat.

I alone was silent.

Perched on a cliff, as it were. Frozen in time. Pondering.

Do I make the leap?

If I do, will I survive to tell the tale?

Nobody ever called me a coward—not if they wanted to live long and prosper, anyhow.

But today I was almost shaking in my shoes and vacillating in the face of the most important decision I would ever make: Do I go in, or not?

If I don't, I know I'll never be back. It will be over for me. The things I have devoted the past three years to will evaporate and be as though they had never happened, and I will return to the life I lived for the 33 years before the change. I'll soon be in prison again, and that's where I'll die, a lonely and abandoned three-strike felon.

But I just might die in this place too, and it would only be justice if I did. By rights I should be dead already, for I had broken the oath I had taken to an Organization whose fundamental rule is simple: *Blood in, blood out.* Before you can join, you must shed blood—kill another human being. If you want out, you will be the one to die, at the hands of those you are swearing an oath to today.

I was out now, and so far I had dodged all the bullets, and by constantly watching my back I had managed to get through my most recent prison term with only a few stab wounds from those who had been sent to inflict The Organization's justice.

That was the trouble now. I was still watching my back—I'll have to watch it for the rest of my life. And inside that auditorium that day, where everyone was singing praises to God for his grace and mercy, was the one man I least wanted to have behind my back, where I couldn't see him.

It hadn't always been that way with Stretch.

Stretch was my homeboy. We grew up in the same neighborhood, fought in the same battles against rival gangs, robbed the same stores, sold the same heroin, smoked the same angel dust. But I hadn't seen him for eight years—not since the day I was ordered to kill him, and almost succeeded.

Still I would recognize him anywhere, even if I could only see the back of his head.

And right now the back of his head glared at me from the last row of chairs in the auditorium, from the seat immediately behind the one empty chair I could see in the place.

What if he was packing heat—a *quete*? What if he

had a Boy Scout knife in his pocket? He was fully capable of ending my life with something less than that.

Did I dare go in and sit down in that chair, right in front of him? Turn my back to him?

I hadn't lived this long by being stupid.

Still, if I didn't go in, how would I ever know whether or not the grace and mercy of God is really all it's cracked up to be? How would I know whether the Holy Spirit really can transform lives or not—whether the past three years that I had devoted to Bible study and prayer had been a mere waste of time and energy or not?

Like I said, nobody ever got away with calling me a coward. Because I never was a coward. No matter what the challenge, I always screwed up my courage and took it. I didn't get to the top of The Organization by shirking dirty or dangerous jobs.

This time, though, if I took the challenge, took the plunge, I wouldn't be relying on my street smarts or the terror I could impose on those around me. I would be relying totally on what I believed about grace, mercy, forgiveness, and the power of God to soften the rock-hard hearts of criminal masterminds.

That's what Stretch had been in his prime, before he got shot in the chest, neck, shoulder, jaw and back—five .38 caliber bullets in him—on my orders. He was the shot caller in our neighborhood, a few years older than me, but a master of gang politics and strategy. If somebody wanted to do a hit against another gang, Stretch was the guy to go to for both advice and permission. He was a true criminal mastermind who grew up in juvie halls, Youth

Authority camps, and foster homes. His mother overdosed in a garage when he was just a little boy, and they never found her body till a week later. When he was a teenager, he saw his own father killed. He didn't have much of a chance at going straight, and when he ended up in county detention, he used the opportunity to learn new criminal skills from his comrades.

More than that, he was tough. He would take on guys bigger than him (and he was pretty big), and just keep coming back for more, no matter how hard he got hit.

That's what finally got him in serious trouble with the people in The Organization. Stretch had had his run, but finally he had to be taught who really called the shots in our barrio.

Now, eight years later, he was no longer the mountain of muscle and sinew he had once been. In surgery after the attempted assassination, he had two strokes that left him partially paralyzed on one side.

But a man needs only one hand to stick a knife into another's jugular, if he knows where to aim. And believe me, Stretch knew where to aim.

The waves of music kept coming. The congregation kept clapping and singing, and people around me were beginning to stare. What's the matter with that big guy? He's afraid to go into a church? He looks so tough. Why won't he go in?

It was now or never.

I took a step, then another, and as it had so often when I was on much different missions, the courage followed the action.

I made it to the end of the row where Stretch was

sitting, then took another step, to the row in front of him.

His head turned just then, and he saw me.

His hands stopped mid-clap.

His eyes locked on me.

His lips knit themselves into a line.

His whole body froze, and I could see him taking a deep breath. I could almost picture fire coming out of his mouth and torching me when he would finally exhale, but I just politely asked to be excused by the people I would have to move past to get to that one seat, and they moved aside to let me in.

I don't remember if I smiled at Stretch or not.

All I remember is what I saw in his eyes as I got closer to him.

His mind was no longer in church.

It was back in the city park we called 57.

Chapter 2

If you want to understand what happened that warm spring night in 1989 in 57 Park, and why I, as a 27-year-old felon with three prison terms behind me, including time locked down on the fifth tier of infamous Folsom Prison, ordered an associate to kill one of my best friends, you need to understand a little about the Northeast Los Angeles world I grew up in.

The northeastern edges of Los Angeles, California are home to some pretty impressive institutions. Dodger Stadium is a little over two miles from my front door. On New Year's Day TV crews from all over the world converge on the Rose Parade, less than five miles east of my house. Cal Tech, NASA's Jet Propulsion Laboratory, and Universal Studios Hollywood are all within eight miles. The world-famous Hollywood sign is less than five miles away.

I was one year old when the first episode of *The Beverly Hillbillies* aired on CBS. The mansion where exterior scenes were shot is about a dozen miles from the house where I grew up, but a world away, in the neighborhood that Will Smith rapped about moving to on *The Fresh Prince of Bel Air*.

Edmundo Ramirez

Life might have turned out very differently for me, had I been raised in a different neighborhood, but I can't blame my parents or my environment for the choices I made. My oldest brother, Manuel, grew up in the same family and went on to college and became a highly-respected teacher, working with troubled youths, trying to help them avoid making the kinds of wrong choices I fell into.

As a young child, I looked up to Manuel, who's about seven years older than me. I tried to emulate him; he was always challenging me to read some of the many books he'd collected in his room, and I enjoyed trying to impress him with what I'd learned. But when he left home, my new hero was Herman, just two years older than me. Unfortunately he was already involved in criminal enterprises, and I began to relish his attention and his stories of living on the edge.

I didn't enjoy the fact that Herman was often violent with me, shoving me around, pushing me down, even giving me a black eye from time to time, but he said he was only doing it in order to toughen me up.

In reality, he probably was taking out his own anger and frustration on me. Our father was a heavy drinker who could be really kind and loving as long as he stayed sober, but when he went on a bender, he'd come home looking for a fight. Herman was his punching bag of choice. In turn, I became Herman's punching bag.

I suppose it didn't bother me too much, because I had already been toughened up by what went on at my grade school.

Our family moved to Glassell Park, a community wedged between Glendale and South Pasadena, when I was six years old, and I began first grade at Glassell Elementary School when I was seven.

It wasn't long before I began to be initiated into the lifestyle of the neighborhood.

Glassell Elementary is a big, two-story stucco building with a red tile roof that was already old when I enrolled.

In a basement beneath the first floor classrooms was the boys' restroom, located in a dark hallway that teachers seldom snooped into. Maybe they were too busy, or maybe they didn't want to know what went on down there. It was impossible for a first-grade boy not to find out, though.

Young as I and my classmates were, we had no idea of the larger forces that wanted to control our neighborhood, but the frightening fact is that our school was located smack dab in the middle of territory claimed by one of L.A.'s most notorious and violent street gangs, The Avenues. If you want to know what they're all about, you can search for "The Avenues Gang" on YouTube and learn more than you probably want to know. They cherish their reputation as the most violent gang in one of America's most violent cities.

Older gang members are always on the lookout for tough young kids they can recruit and turn into weapons to be used in the constant battles with other gangs, and the place they looked at our school was down in that basement.

The first time I noticed a bunch of kids gathered off in a dark corner, I was just curious. I wandered over to see what was going on.

The bigger kids had formed a circle around a couple

of new recruits and were taunting them, egging them on. "You gonna let him say that about you?" a third grader who was taller than all the rest was saying to one of the kids, who was hunkering back in a corner, trying to curl up in a ball. "What are you, a sissy? Come on! Fight! Fight!"

The little boy was crossing his legs and pawing his crotch to keep from wetting his pants as he fought back tears. "Come on!" another boy hissed. "You ain't gonna let him get away with that are you? Are you?"

A boy I thought was in second grade was folding his arms in front of the cowering kid, glaring down his nose at him.

"Come on, you know what you gotta do, or are you just gonna stand there and piss your pants?" a voice from in the shadows said, almost calmly, like the speaker really cared.

That did it. The little kid in the corner put his head down and charged at his antagonist, head butting him right in the gut, knocking him sprawling.

A cheer went up from the spectators, and the circle parted, letting the poor little kid go through to the restroom to relieve himself.

The bell rang then, and everyone went charging up the stairs, back to class, talking and laughing about what had just happened.

Back in Miss Winthrow's class, I sat at my desk replaying what I'd just seen over and over in my mind. It was all I could think about. I have no idea what subject we were supposed to be studying. I'd just gotten my schooling in the way of the street.

One part of me was scared. Would I ever dare to go downstairs to the restroom again?

Another part of me thrilled with excitement.

I'd been in enough brawls in my family with five brothers and four sisters that I knew I could handle myself in a fight. The more I thought about it, the more I wanted a chance to be in the middle of that group of basement *vatos*. The boy who'd been playing the part of the tough-guy bully in the fight I'd just witnessed had been congratulated and clapped on the back by all the others, even after the smaller kid had knocked him down.

It was clear to me what a kid needed to do to have friends, and respect, in this neighborhood. And I knew how to do it.

Oh, and by the way. The tall third grader who was instigating the fight? That was Stretch, the older brother of my best friend in first grade, Jackie.

Chapter 3

Twenty-one years later, Stretch and I would have another encounter, there in the park we called 57. By that time I'd had a lot more schooling in the way of the street, and had become one of the educators about that hard way of life.

In street school, those who misbehave don't get sent to time out, they get killed. In the minds of the teachers, the word merciful is a synonym for coward. Forgiveness is something the weak beg for, but never receive. Grace is what your grandfather closes his eyes and says before dinner, while you're cadging an extra wing or two from the KFC bucket.

By then I'd gotten my education in some of the finest institutions of higher learning in the criminal world. At age 20, I'd done my first stint in the Los Angeles County Jail, the place criminals call Grad School. When the robbery charge against me was dropped for insufficient evidence, I got a get out of jail free card and went back on the streets. I was a free man for a year and a week before getting caught selling PCP and ending up back in the slammer.

I was never a hardcore drug user or pusher. PCP

was something I smoked mainly because everybody around me was getting high on it. I sold it because that was part of my job as a low-level member of the Avenues gang. The guys higher up the chain of command live off the taxes they collect from people they send out on the dangerous streets to sell the stuff. But the only way to work your way up to a position of power is to do the bidding of the people above you.

What I barely realized early on was that the real seat of power for all the gangs operating in our neighborhood was in the prison system. Prisoners on death row and in solitary confinement, men who had killed and maimed as a way of life, and who would never be free on the streets again, were the ones calling all the shots. They were known as Brothers in a prison gang I've chosen to refer to merely as The Organization. It's a shadow organization; simply revealing its existence can get you killed.

From early on I did know enough to realize that The Brothers were the real heroes of our society. They were the ones with enough guts and reputation to strike fear (or put a knife) into the heart of anyone who might dare to look at them sideways.

These were the people us kids were taught to emulate and envy from first grade on.

For our kind, being sent to Folsom Prison was like getting a scholarship to Stanford University. A degree from that hard-time institution was regarded like a PhD in crime.

So in the summer of 1983, just before my twenty-second birthday, I got caught with PCP and ended up in jail again.

In the long run, I might have been better off if they'd kept me longer, but with the backlog of court cases and the systematic overcrowding of the county jails, I was soon put out on the streets again, and that's when PCP got the best of me.

Just a few houses down the street from my house, in early September of 1983, a bunch of us were hanging out, smoking dope—PCP and pot—and drinking whatever someone had been able to steal from a local liquor store or supermarket. It's what we did with ourselves a lot of the time.

By this time I had some pretty good street cred, having been in and out of jail and worked my way into association with some of the toughest toughs around by doing their business for them—whatever that business was. If it required beating someone up, they knew they could rely on me to get the job done. If knives or guns were needed, I was their go-to man, especially if lead was likely to fly. In fact my street name by then was *Bala*, the Spanish word for bullet.

It's hard for a person not involved in that lifestyle to realize just how much shooting was going on in neighborhoods like ours on a daily basis in those days. The term "gangbanging" is tossed around loosely, and some people probably think it means strutting down the street with your crew, pushing street people off the sidewalk.

To those of us living the life, it was literal gang BANGing. It involved gunpowder and bullets flying. We'd cruise the streets, shooting at enemies from big four-door cars like the 1962 Chevy Impala I was driving the day my good friend Pete got shot sitting next to me.

It had happened a couple years before I first ended up in jail. Four of us homies had been sitting at the end of one of the many dead-end streets that run up into the hills of our barrio, smoking PCP and drinking, when one of our home girls sauntered up to us. She was the girlfriend of my closest friend, Cholo Mike. In fact they'd had a son together. Mike was in jail at the time, and I guess she was out looking for friends—or maybe for trouble. "Hey, what you guys doing?" she said.

"Nothin'."

"You got some dope. Come on, let me get high with you."

"Nah. Get lost!"

She backed away, looking hurt. "Mike would let me."

"You heard me, get lost!" I shouted. "Go take care of his kid like a good momma. You want me to tell him you're out here cruisin' the streets lookin' to get laid?"

She got all pouty, but just stood there, maybe hoping we'd relent and let her have some angel dust, but we weren't interested, and it wouldn't be right to hit on a friend's girl while he was incapacitated.

We all just turned our backs on her, sitting there on the trunk of my car.

"So, what you gonna do?" she whined.

"We ain't gonna DO nothin'." I yelled without turning around. "Soon as we're done here, I'm takin' Victor home, then I'm goin' home and goin' to bed. So get lost!"

She turned then and I heard her feet scuffing on the loose gravel scattered on the pavement. "What a bitch," I complained to my buddies, and they all nodded their agreement. "I don't get what Mike sees in her."

Mike was about the smartest guy I knew—in both street smarts and book learning. A very talented guy, who could have done most anything with his life, if he'd chosen to live on the right side of the law. As teenagers he and I had hung out together a lot. His house was just down the street and around the corner from mine, and he seemed to have everything going for him. His dad had a good-paying job working for the Rapid Transit District, and in their garage he had a woodworking shop where he built jewelers' tables for sale. As young teens Mike and I spent most of our free time there learning how to build things with wood.

Unfortunately we got another kind of education there, too, because Mike's uncle was an Organization operator who bought and sold heroin in large quantities. When Mike's dad wasn't there, the uncle would have his customers come by to shoot up and smoke the stuff.

Soon I was good enough at building the jewelers' tables that Mike's dad would pay me $40 for each one I built, and I began spending that money on his uncle's products. Mike did too, and that's probably why he ended up getting his higher education in jail rather than at USC or UCLA.

With Mike in jail, I spent my time running with Pete, Victor, and Anthony, strong-arming, selling dope, chasing rival gang operators out of the hood, and enforcing the will of people higher up the gang ladder. It was dangerous work, but we liked what we were doing, and thrilled to the adrenaline it kept pumping through our systems.

Edmundo Ramirez

We were about to get more of a rush than we'd bargained for, though.

Chapter 4

Watching the sunset fade on the San Gabriel Mountains to the north and east could be a real trip if you had enough PCP in your system, so the four of us stayed there, slouching on the trunk of my beat-up old Impala, enjoying the show till it got dark and we started feeling cold. "Come on, let's get you home," I said to Victor, who lived down one hill, up over another, and back in a narrow alley.

We stumbled into the car. Considering the condition I was in, it's a good thing all the roads on the way to his house were narrow, winding ones where I wouldn't be driving very fast.

After we dropped Victor off, I had to go down a narrow street, then turn into an especially narrow alley.

As soon as we turned that corner, doors on every side started opening, and in the dim light we became instantly aware that the people coming out were not our friends. Immediately I realized we'd probably been set up. People knew we were coming, and were waiting for us.

I didn't have to say a thing to Pete or Anthony. In a

flash we all had our doors open, and were out in the alley facing down members of a rival gang.

At first it was just fists flying, and a lot of pushing and shoving, trying to bash each other's heads against a wall, but as more and more of our enemies entered the fray, the three of us realized this was a no-win situation, and we made a dash for the car. Pete slid into the seat beside me and Anthony jumped into the back seat. We slammed our doors, and I gunned the engine.

That's when the guns came out, and I began to hear lead smashing into my beloved ride.

"I'm hit!" Pete screamed suddenly, then he slumped over against me.

In the dim light I looked down, and I could see blood pulsing out of his right arm.

Just as I lowered my head for a closer look, a bullet slammed through the driver's window and into my windshield and landed on the dashboard. I realized that if I hadn't looked down just when I did, the bullet would have hit me in the back of the head, probably ending my life.

I floored it, not caring if anyone or anything was in front of me, and squealed around the next corner, headed for Glendale Memorial Hospital.

I never looked in my rearview mirror all the way there, but another car must have followed us most of the way, because I kept hearing gunfire behind us.

It seems hard to believe, in this day of everyone having a cell phone to call 911, that when I was growing up teenagers would drive up and down the streets shooting at each other on a regular basis, but that's the life we lived, and the police almost never caught up with us before the shooting was over. I have no idea how many innocent people were caught in the crossfire, or how much property damage was done, but that sort of activity was the definition of gang banging in those days. It wasn't until a massive secret meeting of leaders of all the gangs was held in 1992 in Elysian Park that word came down to everyone from The Organization that drive-by shootings would no longer be tolerated.

I roared into the emergency area of the hospital and ran in, shouting that my friend had been shot. The staff there was very good, and came running out and soon had him in treatment where they were able to stop the bleeding.

Of course they also called the police.

"Who shot your friend?" the officer who responded asked me over and over again.

"I don't know!" I declared. "We were just out cruising, and all of a sudden somebody started shooting at us. We never even saw where the bullets were coming from!"

The officer looked down at my skinned-up knuckles and the bruises on my face from the fight before the shooting started. "Son, I can help you, but you've got to help me first," he said in a gruff voice.

"Honest officer, I've never seen anything like this before! I don't know what happened, why they wanted to start shooting at us. It must be some of those gangs you hear about, but I don't know nothin' about them."

He looked me up and down and shook his head and shrugged. "You better go call your friend's family."

These days he would have gone to his cruiser, typed my name and Pete's name into a computer, and seen

Edmundo Ramirez

that we were both men with criminal records who were associating with each other, and would have hauled me in for further questioning. But he was probably an overworked beat cop who didn't want to spend the next three days doing paperwork on me, so he turned and walked away.

I went into the hospital and called Pete's mom. The doctors got Pete stabilized, then sent him over to the USC Hospital for further treatment.

The bullet had gone into Pete's right shoulder and traveled down to his right elbow. It's still there to this day, 25 years later, because removing it would have done more damage to his arm. As it was, the arm was paralyzed and Pete, who worked as a draftsman in the days when all drafting was done by hand, was in a very bad situation.

In the end, the events of that horrible day would turn out to be a blessing in disguise, I guess. But at the time I felt terrible for getting one of my closest friends into such a fix. Pete and I went back a long ways, and had spent a lot of time gang banging together.

But worse days were yet to come, and as my life descended into a living hell, I finally decided I'd had enough of the rough street life and resolved to turn things around once and for all, get a real job, and leave my banging associates behind.

Just one more party, and I'd be done with all that kind of thing forever.

Chapter 5

I felt bad about Pete getting shot, but with enough time I was able to rationalize that it was just part of the business we were involved in. People were getting shot and stabbed and beat up all the time. It was just a cost of doing business.

And, because Pete was seen as the victim of senseless gang violence, a fund set up for victims of violent crime sponsored him to get training in a profession that he could practice even with a paralyzed arm. By 1983 he was working as a DJ at a local radio station, KGLH.

One summer night, about the time I turned 22, he and I were drinking and socializing at a bar on Verdugo Avenue with some of our homies. Cholo Mike, my best friend from school and the woodworking shop, wasn't with us, but he and his girlfriend came by on their way home from a movie and stayed and visited for a while. Pete and I and two friends stayed till the bar closed at 2 A. M, then started walking home. Actually the house where I grew up was all torn down, waiting to be rebuilt at the time, and my folks were living a couple miles away, but there was a little camper parked on the property, where I would spend the night if I didn't feel like going all the way to my folks' house.

It would take me probably twenty-five minutes to get to the camper, and I could get at least a little sleep before I had to report for work with the construction company I was working for at that time. I'd been working for the same company off and on for several years. My brother Herman got me the job when I was fifteen, and whenever I was out of jail, they would hire me back, because one of the things Herman taught me was to work really hard whenever I was given a job.

When the four of us got to Verdugo Market, we heard the alarm going off. Somebody had kicked in the front door, but we just kept on walking—didn't want to be there when the police arrived. A couple blocks later we turned a corner and one of my friends decided to "head up" a wall with the Avenues' gang tag. While he was doing that, a police squad car turned the corner, headed our way. Pete and the other two took off running, but I had just finished serving a several-week sentence in county jail for drunk driving, and figured my slate was clean with the law, so I just kept walking.

The squad car pulled up beside me, and the officer on the passenger side got out and asked to see my driver's license. He used the information to fill out a Field I. D. card, identifying me as a gang member. Then he made me put my hands behind my back and handcuffed me and told me to get into the car. "Where we goin' man?," I asked. "I got no warrants."

He didn't bother to answer, just shut the door on me and got back in. The driver pulled a U-turn, and we went back to the Verdugo Market. "What do you know about this?" I was asked as they got me out of the car.

"I don't know nothin'! The alarm was going off when I walked past."

"Right, so I don't suppose we'll find any of your fingerprints in there, huh?"

"You got it, man. I didn't have nothin' to do with that."

They weren't willing to take that for an answer, but I kept reaffirming my innocence and told them they could check at the bar up the street—the bartender knew my friends and I had stayed till closing time. We hadn't had time to break into the store.

Frustrated, they shoved me back into the car and drove half a block north on Verdugo, then got me out and took the cuffs off. "You head on home, then, boy."

"Yes, sir, officer. That's where I'm heading," I said as diplomatically as I could muster, then started walking south on Verdugo, toward Avenue 33, where I would make a left turn and head over toward the place I'd grown up.

"Hey!" the officer in the passenger seat yelled through his open window. "That's the wrong direction. You don't live that way, now turn around and walk the other way!"

I had no choice but to stop, turn around, and start walking north. They seemed really intent on making sure I went that way, and cruised along beside me for a block or so, until we were beside the ball fields at Glassell Park. Then the driver gunned the engine and took off.

As soon as they were gone, I heard a sound off to my left.

Edmundo Ramirez

It's a sound like no other. I'd recognize it anywhere.
The sound of guns being cocked.

Slowly I turned my head and found myself staring into the shadows where I could barely make out the form of three men. One of them had what appeared to be a deer hunting rifle, the other two had pistols, and all three of the barrels were pointed right at me.

Your internal clock starts spinning like a top when you're in that kind of situation. Everything around you seems to slow down. Some people see their whole life flash before them in less than a second.

For me, I didn't have time for a lifetime movie. My whirling mind was too busy calculating how long it would be before those guys started shooting.

I was pretty good at those kinds of calculations, and it paid off. Just when I figured the bullets were about to fly, I leapt into action and started running down the street. The first reports followed me, but I'd moved at just the right instant to literally dodge the bullets.

My luck held out for several seconds, but when I was about a hundred feet down the sidewalk, I felt something like a sledge hammer hit me on the right side.

A bullet entered my back, tore through my right side, and ripped out beside my hip, taking a big chunk of flesh with it. Instantly, searing pain flooded my body, but I didn't dare stop. I kept running as best I could, with bullets whizzing past on either side of me. Finally I came to a place where a hedge grew beside the road, and I somehow pushed my way through and hunkered down behind the bushes.

The shooters weren't far behind me, but in the dim

light they couldn't see where I had gone. I couldn't see them either, but I could hear their footsteps, and when I heard them turn the corner and go running up a side street, I figured they weren't coming back. Still I hid there for several minutes, just to be sure.

The cops, for their part, couldn't have helped but hear the gunfire, but they didn't bother to come back and check on what was going on. To this day I believe I was set up, by the police, to be killed by rival gang members that night. It wasn't necessarily that the police were working in cahoots with the other guys, maybe they just figured that dropping me off there was the easiest way to get one more tough guy off the streets for good.

I, and every gang member I knew, had experienced things like that before. Whenever we ended up in jail, it seemed like standard operating procedure to put us in a holding tank with our sworn enemies. Would anyone on the force care if one of us got killed? I don't think so. It would just make their jobs easier.

Easier yet if we got killed on a dark street at 3 A. M. Less mess to clean up; fewer uncooperative witnesses to interrogate.

Finally I crawled out onto the sidewalk and began to limp toward the nearest friend's house that I could think of, hoping someone there would give me a ride to the hospital.

I pounded on the door till I woke up my friend Dynicio. When his wife heard the commotion, she came out and asked what had happened. She wanted to see the wound, and when she did, she started screaming and crying hysterically. "You gotta get to the hospital, Bullet. Quick!"

That took me by surprise. I hadn't even looked at the wound yet; I'd just been trying to hold myself together and staunch the bleeding with my hand, but she could see that I was losing blood pretty fast, and that a big chunk of flesh was dangling by a thread. I think it must have been a bullet from the hunting rifle that hit me. In fact, that's what the doctor who sewed me up later told me it probably was.

Dynicio woke up another friend who was crashing there at his pad and told him to give me a ride to the hospital. The guy fumbled around for his keys, half awake, probably stoned, then led me down to his car. Once we were seated, though, he just sat there with his hands on the steering wheel, staring straight ahead.

"Come on, let's go, man," I said.

He continued staring straight ahead.

"Come on, man. I'm dying here."

"What if they come back?"

"So that's it, you're ranking out on me?"

"I can't get my car shot up."

"Damn," was all I could say as I pushed the door open and rolled out, barely able to stand.

Somehow I managed to walk the mile, up a gradual hill, to Mike's house. Pounding on the door with what little strength I had left, I managed to wake his mother up. "Can you wake Mike up and have him take me to the hospital?" I pled.

"He's gotta get his rest, he's got work today," she said. "Besides, if we wake the baby, nobody else will get any sleep for the rest of the night. I'll call Playboy and your dad, have them take you to the hospital.

Playboy was Mike's older brother, who lived nearby.

I don't know whether I didn't hear her say that, or whether I was just too out of it from loss of blood by then, but I just turned and walked back down to the street and headed up the steep hill toward the trailer where I figured I could at least lay down, and maybe die in peace.

I almost made it, but within sight of my goal, I collapsed face first on the sidewalk. That's where Playboy and my dad found me.

I woke up the next day in the hospital, in excruciating pain, and with a lot to think about.

The events of that night set things in motion in my life that could have led to something really good. Instead they led me into the worst day of my life so far.

Chapter 6

As I lay on the hospital bed, coming out from under the haze of alcohol, angel dust, and pain killers, the reality of what had happened to me settled on my chest like a lead blanket.

I wavered between consciousness and unconsciousness, wracked with pain that washed over me, making it impossible to think. Finally, after a day or two, I really don't know how long, I came fully awake to a stark reality, cold sweat dripping off my face and chest.

I was just twenty-one years old. Where was my life going? Where could it go from here?

I was a tough guy who acted like he ruled his little corner of the world, but what had happened to me forced me to realize that I was really just a pawn on a chess board controlled by much larger players, many of whom would take my life at the drop of a hat if they were told to, or if I just happened to be in the wrong place at the wrong time. What were the chances I would live to see my twenty-second birthday?

As an enforcer for my gang, I had often used a gun on others. My street name was Bullet. I had seen friends and associates get shot. I'd watched some of them die, and I'd taken vengeance, evening the score, making sure those who hurt my people were soon hurting worse. But being on the receiving end of gunfire—at last running out of luck and failing to dodge the bullet coming my way—that put life and death in a whole new perspective.

Enveloped in pain and perspiration, I had one of the first moments of true perspicuity in my life (not that I had ever heard the word *perspicuity* at the time, or would have known what it meant, had I heard it. I hadn't paid much attention in school. My chosen career path didn't require getting good grades.)

Now the life I had lived passed like a newsreel through my consciousness, starting with the fights in the school basement. That's where I'd earned my first stripes, as the older guys, who were controlled by older guys yet, watched me fight. They could tell that I was cut from the same cloth as my brother Herman. I would take on anyone and never back down, even after getting knocked down, even if blood was gushing from my nose. I just kept coming back for more, till whoever they had pitted against me that day threw in the towel.

Later I was one of the older guys watching the fights, urging the little kids on. Then for some reason that extracurricular activity was curtailed, maybe by the teachers, I don't know for sure. But when I got to junior high, the people who had been watching me came by to remind me that they had already "jumped me in," and that I was part of their branch of the Avenues Gang. In grade school the guys chosen by the gang had been called Baby Avenues. Now we were to be known as Tiny Locos, and we were to hang with each other, and with the older Avenues, not with anyone else.

We were watched all through school, and those of us who survived, and whose families didn't move us to a new neighborhood to interrupt our downward path, earned our rank in the outfit by being tough, selling drugs, and collecting taxes for the power brokers above us. We learned the basic rules of gang life— that to show cowardice was a fatal flaw, that snitches end up in ditches (dead), that you always backed up your homies, that an insult to any member had to be avenged, and in turn if you were insulted or injured, your boys would have your back and deliver retribution.

Retribution was one of my specialties.

My boys and I, by time we were in high school, had a street reputation that if anybody dared cross us, we'd make sure they lived long enough to regret it, but sometimes not much longer. To us, as teenagers, it seemed like a game. But it was literally a life-and-death game. Any of us could have been killed by rivals at any moment, and some of us were. Gang violence in our part of the city was so common in those days that many killings never made the evening news and got barely any mention, even in local newspapers.

Now, here I was, out of school, living the tough guy life, doing enforcement for people whose orders came down from I didn't know where. But right now I didn't feel very tough at all.

I thought back over the number of friends and associates I'd lost—some of them killed, others injured so badly they could never cruise with me again, others with long prison sentences.

Edmundo Ramirez

Nobody I knew of, who was living this life, had made it much past thirty as a free man or woman.

As a kid, I had dreamed of living this life. It seemed so glamorous.

Now reality was settling in.

Constantly having to watch your back, constantly wondering who is drawing a bead on you from a passing car or a nearby apartment building, always having to play the tough guy against young kids in your own gang who were just waiting for you to mess up so they could take over your territory. It wasn't really much fun at all. There must be something more to life than this. Maybe my brother Manuel could help me. He'd gone to college. He was a teacher now. I needed to talk to him, find out how to start life over and live on the right side of the law. As soon as I regained some strength and was able to be up and around, I would start a new life. Maybe get married. Have a family, live out in the suburbs somewhere safe where my homies would never find me. I'd need to move someplace far away, I knew that. Once I'd been jumped into the gang, I'd made a life commitment. More than one of my friends had paid the ultimate price for turning his back on his brotherhood.

I would make it work, though. I had to. I couldn't go on like this, waiting every day for a bullet or knife blade to find its lethal mark in me.

Chapter 7

When I went home from the hospital, it was to one of my sisters' places about twenty minutes' drive from the old neighborhood. I have four sisters and five brothers. I'm number eight of ten children.

On the property where I grew up, a new house was taking shape. The lot was at the end of a dead end street, up on a hill, and through the years the hill had begun to shift, cracking the foundation. So my parents arranged with the construction company I'd been working for since I was fifteen to come in, tear the old house down, take out the foundation, drive piers into the ground for support, and then pour a new foundation. On that foundation we built a first story, then brought in a house that had been condemned because a freeway was being built and it had to be either torn down or moved, and set it on top of the first story.

By time I was ready to go back to work a month or so after I got out of the hospital, the construction project was wrapping up, and my parents and two younger brothers had moved into the new house. I continued to live with my sister in Alhambra, driving to the construction site every day in my '72 Chevy pickup.

I had a lot of time to think while I was recovering, and while I worked on the house. In my mind I kept formulating plans for somehow escaping the war zone of Northeast Los Angeles. I knew I had to do it, I just wasn't sure how. The break would come, I knew, after the house was finished.

I couldn't tell anyone else, not even my closest friends, what I was thinking—it wouldn't be safe. When the day came for me to make my move, I would have to do it all on my own—just disappear one day and leave no trace, no forwarding address, no way for even my family to find me.

No one I know of collects statistics on how many gang-related murders are inside jobs, brother against brother, but those living the life know it's a high percentage. Your brothers are supposed to stand up for you, but if you cross the wrong line, orders will come down from above, and your closest friend may be the one given the assignment to "deal with" you.

It was on September 11, 1983, just two months after my twenty-second birthday, that we nailed the last shingle to the roof.

That deserved a celebration. That, plus the fact that starting tomorrow I would put into motion the plans I had been working out.

One last party, then I'd be gone. I'd just disappear, find a new place to live, start life over.

I went to my sister's house, got cleaned up, then out onto the street with some of my buddies, drinking, smoking PCP, and hanging out. Pretty soon one of the guys suggested we go back to the neighborhood, and it seemed like a good idea. There'd be more homies to hang with there, so I loaded four or five guys into the back of my pickup, and a couple more in the cab, and off we went.

In the neighborhood, just a couple blocks from my folks' property, was an abandoned house that had a huge tree in the front yard that covered most of the street—the perfect dark corner to party on a warm summer evening.

There was a lot of alcohol involved, and a lot of PCP; probably eighteen or twenty people there all together, talking, laughing, sometimes fighting—but mostly in good fun. This was to be the party of my life. My one last *vorlo* before I got serious and turned over a new leaf. I was determined to do as much booze and angel dust as I could—have a really good time, one last time.

Soon I was in such a haze—almost a stupor—that I had no idea what was going on around me. I've tried and tried to recall what went down, but my brain was fried. All I know is that I suddenly came out of la-la land to the sound of my best friend Mike screaming, a blood-curdling scream. "Mundo! Mundo! Bala! I been shot! I been shot!"

The smell of burned powder and sulfur hung in the air.

Someone had shot Mike in the stomach. He was doubled over, screaming in pain. I didn't know what had happened, but I knew what I had to do. I ran to him. "Come on, we've got to get you to the hospital!" I screamed.

He could barely walk, so I helped him to my truck, half carrying him, and sat him in the passenger seat, then ran around and tore out, headed for the nearest emergency room.

I could tell he was hurt bad, so I raced down the hill, turned left on Cazador, headed for San Fernando Road. As we sped past the grade school Mike and I had attended together, my lifelong friend was screaming in pain, "O God, help me God, help me God!"

I remember thinking as I drove madly up San Fernando Road to the hospital, What do I know about God? How can I help my homie? How can God help my homie? Oh God, please help him!

My religious experience up to that day had consisted of an occasional visit to Saint Bernard's Catholic Church. My grandmothers were both very religious, always saying prayers and doing the rosary, but all that religion stuff never meant anything to me. In the world I inhabited, religion was for cowards.

In my desperation now, though, I wished I knew how to talk to God, how to get him to do something for my homeboy. All I could think of to do was go to the church and maybe light some candles for him or something.

We roared up to the emergency entrance, and soon Cholo Mike was under the care of people who knew what to do.

The police were there, too, with their questions about what had happened.

"I don't know, officers," was my plea. "We were at a liquor store together, and Mike went outside to relieve himself. I heard two shots and ran out to see what was going on, and there he was, down on the sidewalk, bleeding and screaming in pain. I didn't see who did it, honest I didn't see nothin'."

A crowd was gathering in the waiting room. Mike's grandparents/parents were there by then (Mike had been raised by his grandparents, who had adopted him, so they were technically both his grandparents and his parents.) Playboy, his brother/uncle who had helped me when I got shot, was there as well, and people who had been at the party were starting to come in.

I watched as the police started interviewing other witnesses. I could see them glancing my way from time to time, sometimes pointing, but I didn't care. I knew nobody would snitch about what had really happened.

What had happened? I wondered.

I honestly didn't know.

All I could think of was God, please help my friend. Please help him live. You know I'm going to go straight now, but please, help Mike too! He's such a good guy. He's got such a great future, if he can just get his life straightened out. God, please help him! Please!

Chapter 8

Mike was in surgery for several hours. Finally I was so tired I knew I needed to go and get some rest, so I headed for my parents' house. When I turned on Avenue 33 and went past Saint Bernard's, I saw that the front door was open. I really should go in and light a candle for Mike, I thought. But by then I was so exhausted I couldn't make myself do anything but go to the house, take a shower, wash Mike's blood down the drain, and crawl into bed.

I lay there for a long time, waves of remorse sweeping over me. Why had I chosen to party that night? What had I done? Was it possible I might have hurt my friend? What would happen to him? What would happen to his little boy? What would happen to me?

Finally I fell asleep on a tear-soaked pillow.

In the morning the phone rang. It was Mike's grandma/mom. You better get to the hospital," she said.

My sister Maggie was there, and she offered to drive me—she could see I was in no shape to get behind the wheel.

A crowd of friends and family were still there in the waiting area, talking quietly, some of them weeping.

"What's happening?" I asked Mike's dad, the man who had taught me woodworking skills even before I was a teenager, who I loved and respected like a second father.

"Very bad. Very bad. Not good at all," was all he could say.

Then we heard the Code Blue. We looked at each other. Fear washed through the room.

An hour later a doctor came out and asked to speak to the parents. They went to a quiet corner, and a moment later his mom screamed and collapsed into her husband's arms. We knew then what the news was.

I was numb, in shock. All I could do is say "I'm sorry, I'm so, so sorry" as I wept uncontrollably. Mike and I had been so close—he was the dearest person to me in the world. We'd done everything together, and now he was gone.

My sister Maggie put her arm around me. We were both weeping uncontrollably. Finally she said, "There's nothing more we can do here. Let me take you home."

On the long ride to Maggie's apartment in Alhambra, all I could think of is Mike is gone. He's gone. My best friend in the world. He's gone. Why didn't I stop and light a candle for him? It was the least I could have done. Maybe God would have helped him. Maybe he'd still be here.

I sat, numb, in Maggie's living room, and then the pain hit me again, and I broke down. Tough guy Bullet crying like an abandoned baby, weeping uncontrollably. How had my life come to this? The night had started out with so much promise. Today was to be the day ...

Finally I stumbled up the stairs to my sister Katy's apartment, the place I'd been staying.

I lay down on my bed, but I was so strung out there was no way I could sleep. She had some sleeping pills, so I took several. I wanted somehow to escape the nightmare I was living in, but sleep would not come. I lay there sobbing, thinking, asking myself what had gone wrong.

Today was supposed to be the day I would begin a new, better life.

I would begin a new life, that was true. But not the one I had planned.

Chapter 9

As I lay on my bed, miserable, strung out on PCP that I had smoked sometime between the time I took Mike to the hospital and now, with my mind deadened by sleeping pills, I heard the phone ringing somewhere off in the far distance.

A moment later Katy was tapping on my door. "Yeah," was all I could muster.

"It's Dad," she said as she handed me the phone.

"The detectives are here," Dad said. "They want to ask you a few more questions. Are you going to be okay if we come there to see you?"

"Yeah, Dad."

"They want you to go downtown with them."

My heart almost stopped.

"You okay?" Dad asked.

"Okay." What else could I say?

"We'll be there in a few minutes."

My head was swimming in drugs, confusion, sorrow, and fear. I couldn't speak.

"You okay, Mundo?" Katy

"Yeah."

I let the phone fall on the bed.

More questions? What could I tell them? I didn't have any answers. All I had was questions.

It seemed like only a few minutes till there was a knock at Katy's door. "Hey Dad," I said when I saw my dad standing there by himself, his head hanging.

"They're downstairs," he said.

"Okay."

"You ready?"

"They want me to go downtown?"

"Yes."

Downtown in detective-talk meant Parker Center, what people called The Glass House. The place you'd sometimes see Lieutenant Joe Friday in front of in *Dragnet* reruns. When it first opened in 1954, it was called the Police Administration Building, but when L. A. Police Chief William H. Parker died of a heart attack in1966, the city council renamed it The Parker Center in his memory. It served as the headquarters for the LAPD until 2009.

The eight-story building housed most of the administrative offices for the police department, a crime lab, interview rooms, and most significantly for me, the headquarters for a C.R.A.S.H. unit. Every police division in L. A. had a C.R.A.S.H. unit assigned to it.

Originally called T.R.A.S.H., when it was instituted in 1973, the acronym stood for Total Resources Against Street Hoodlums. By my time it had been re-named less-pejoratively Community Resources Against Street Hoodlums.

I knew from experience that my police record qualified me to be subjected to the harsh treatment the units meted out against Street Hoodlums. The detectives, uniformed police, and undercover operators assigned to these units specialized in knowing everything there was to know about each and every person known to have gang affiliations, which of course included me.

Fifteen years later, the highly-publicized Ramparts Scandal centered on the operations of crooked C.R.A.S.H. cops who crossed the line into criminal activity themselves while supposedly cleaning up the streets. If you've ever watched the FX Network show *The Shield,* you have an idea of how the Ramparts Division C.R.A.S.H. unit operated. Eventually it came out that officers there had planted evidence, used extortion, and just about any method they could to get convictions, all the while running their own illegal drug operation on the side, selling crack cocaine stolen from evidence lockers.

I knew what was in store for me if I went downtown. But what choice did I have?

"Let's go," I said, shuffling out the door.

We walked down the steps from the second floor together.

In the parking lot was a big, black Crown Victoria—a detective car.

The detectives cuffed me, read me my rights, then put Dad and me in the back seat of their car.

We went to my folks' house first, to drop Dad off. He and I didn't talk on the way there. I just hung my head, trying to keep it together. There was nothing I could think of to tell him. When he got out, I said "I love you, Dad."

"I love you too, son." Then he hung his head and shuffled toward the front door of the brand new house we had just finished building. What a horrible house-warming gift I had brought him!

On the way downtown the detectives said absolutely nothing to me. I was left alone with my thoughts and sorrow for what had happened, and my dread of what was about to happen.

We pulled into the back lot at Parker Center, and the detectives got me out and took me in through a back door. In a hallway on the way to the interview room, they made sure that I saw a bunch of my homies lined up, waiting for their turn in the question box. It was a wise strategic move. Understanding gang mentality as well as they did, they knew that seeing my Avenues brothers there would plant the idea of a confession in my mind, no matter whether I'd actually committed a crime or not. They knew it would make it easier for me to do the "honorable" thing and take the rap for what had happened, to spare my home boys. That would earn me points on The Organization's scorecard.

The next five hours were living hell.

Because they had spent much of their careers dealing with street toughs who never caved easily, CRASH officers had developed techniques for breaking through the hard outer skin we all wore.

I was already emotionally spent. My best friend had just died, and I couldn't help but wonder whether I had been the one to pull the trigger. Guilt and grief competed for the honor of breaking me down. Then they came at me with fists and slaps.

In addition to the physical abuse, they used every psychological trick in their book, telling me that others had ratted on me, saying I'd shot Mike in a fit of rage, threatening me with the death penalty if they could prove premeditated intent and that there had been a drug deal involved. Newspapers were already reporting the incident as a drug deal gone south. What did I want the rest of my life to be? Clinging to life in a death row cell, sending appeals up the judicial ladder till I ran out of options? Or maybe life in prison without the possibility of parole would be my choice? What did I want out of life, they kept asking me.

My options on September 12 were so different than the new, clean life I had been dreaming about on September 11.

I was devastated.

So much had changed in the split second it took for someone to pull a trigger twice.

I held out for several hours, but finally I couldn't take any more.

When one of my interrogators, the one playing "good cop" against the abusive guy's "bad cop," started talking about the possibility of a plea deal, maybe involuntary manslaughter, if I'd just cooperate, I broke.

"All right, all right. I'll tell you what happened!" I shouted.

"Good. That's what I want to hear," he said. "You'll feel so much better once you get it off your chest."

"But you've got to let my homies go."

"I can't make any promises, but..."

"Let them go, or I don't talk!" I stared into his eyes, cold as ice, and he must have sensed that this was as far as he could get me to go.

"I'll see what I can do."

I turned and stared at the wall. We sat like that for

several minutes, waiting to see who would break and speak first. Finally he got up and left the room without saying anything.

What seemed like a long time later, he came back. "This better be good," he said. "You tell me what really happened, they're free to go."

I didn't know whether to trust him, but I figured if I made the story good enough—bad enough for me, that is—he wouldn't have any reason to hold the others.

I looked down at the table and began the story. "We were partying. Just hanging out. Smoking dope. Drinking. You know how it is."

"I think I do."

"I was just fooling around, twirling this pistol around, getting really loaded up with drugs and alcohol, and the next thing I knew, I turned around and started shooting at my pickup truck."

"At your truck?"

I hung my head and broke down in tears, laid my head on my arms on the table. "I didn't know Mike was on the other side. I had no idea. He was my best friend, since we were little kids. I'd never do anything to hurt him. Never."

"But he's dead, isn't he?"

I nodded without lifting my head.

"And you killed him."

"It was an accident. Just a *#&/*! accident. I never would have pulled the trigger if I'd known he was there."

"Thank you, Mundo," the detective said. "It feels good to get that off your chest, doesn't it?"

I nodded again without lifting my head.

"I'm going to go type up your statement and get you

to sign it," he said as he left the room. The door closing sounded to me like a prison gate.

Alone again, I sat there, head on my arms, and sobbed.

Chapter 10

I was booked into the Los Angeles County Jail, charged with murder, on September 12, 1983, the day I had planned to make a clean break with my criminal past.

If only I hadn't decided to get high and party one last time, how different my life could have been.

I went through the booking process in a daze, feeling like I had been hit by a train.

It was one thing to be promised a deal by a cop, quite another to get a judge, jury, and the district attorney to agree to your plea. I knew that the police will promise you almost anything to get you to cooperate, even if it isn't something that's in their power to deliver.

But at that point I didn't have the emotional energy to care. My life had completely come apart at the seams in a way that could never be mended. My best friend was dead, and everybody in the neighborhood probably hated me by now, because the story going around was that I was the one who'd shot him.

I stumbled through the motions of getting booked in, then they put me in an elevator and took me upstairs to the glass house within the glass house. I'd been there before, so I knew what to expect.

They take you off the elevator and make you take all your clothes off for a strip search, right where all the guys already detained in a hundred-person holding cell can watch, then they give your street clothes back and open the one door into that huge room stacked with bunk beds and open-air toilets and enclosed by inch-thick shatterproof glass.

I stood tall as I walked into that fish tank, looking around me, daring anyone to meet my eyes, but all the while secretly hoping and praying that I wouldn't meet any familiar faces—at least not faces of people I'd had to enforce against in the past. It wasn't uncommon to meet guys from your own gang, or from a rival gang, in a holding cell. Experience taught you to form alliances right away. You needed someone to watch your back if you didn't want to get stabbed in your sleep.

Fortunately there wasn't anyone there I was sure I needed to worry about. It was mainly blacks, a few whites, and some Mexicans from far enough out of my hood that I'd never crossed them, so I went quietly to my assigned bunk. I was entirely too drained to put any energy into socializing.

I sat there for a long time, bemoaning what had happened to me. Fate seemed to have entirely turned against me. Why on this day, of all days, the day I was supposed to free myself of my past, had fate chosen to drive me face to face with the darkest side of my nature?

While I was still immersed in my private misery, I heard the elevator bell ring. More customers were being brought to the glass motel.

I watched with little interest as the doors slid open, and then my heart dropped.

There were five guys inside, along with a police escort, and I recognized all of them.

I had gone to school with them, in junior high.

But they weren't Avenues. They were Frogtown. The one gang that never could get along with the other crews represented at our school. They'd been the outcasts then, and they didn't care a bit. In fact they relished their reputation for being on the outside of every alliance.

Now I began to wish with all my heart that I could have found some allies in the tank before they arrived.

All I could do now was keep my head down and hope not to be noticed.

Fat chance that would work in a glass castle.

The five of them strolled into the cage together after they'd been put on display for all of us during the strip search. It was time for them to recover some of their dignity, so their posse moved about together, ready to wrest control of choice bunks from anyone who blinked.

Oscar, their leader, sat down on a bunk directly across from me. "Where you from home boy?" he said, not because he was interested in hearing me talk about my background.

I raised my head slowly, till I could look right into his eyes. "Avenues."

"Thought so." He looked around at his crew, then slowly raised himself to his feet. His boys gathered around him, eyes fixed on me as he started to advance.

I got to my feet too. I knew I was no match for five

toughs, but I'd never backed down from a fight in my life, and I could see no reason to start now. What did I have to lose? Being knocked out or even killed would at least release me from my pain.

"Hey Mundo, that you?" a voice from the back of the pack asked just as Oscar and I were about to come to blows.

"Yeah, man, Gilbert! It's me," I said as soon as I recognized his voice.

"Hey, he's cool compadre" Gilbert said to Oscar. "This is the guy I was telling you about, remember? When I was at that party about to get my face pounded into the slab by the Aves. Mundo stood up for me, didn't you Mundo?"

"Yeah, I had your back, man."

All of us had gone to school together at one time, but we'd never been friends. But one time when Gilbert was falling for an Avenues girl, he came to a party, and a bunch of my guys were ready to teach him a lesson, but I stood up and told them to back off.

Oscar took a step back and looked me over, then extended his hand. Each of them came forward then and shook my hand.

When we sat down again, Oscar said, "So, what they got you for, ese?" (Ese, pronounced "s.a." is a Spanish word gang members often address each other with, it's simply a way of getting someone else's attention.)

"Mike got shot," they're tryna pin it on me."

"Mike? No. You didn't do it, did you? You'd never shoot him, man I know that."

"I'm copping to it—involuntary. Save my boys some trouble."

"No kiddin' man. That's right noble of you man. But Mike, poor guy. He gonna be okay?"

I let my head fall forward, shaking it as I stared at the floor. "He's not dead man? Not Mike!" Gilbert said, coming over and squatting down beside me.

I didn't respond.

"Oh man, that's awful."

They walked away then and left me alone. In fact, during the three days I spent there, the Frogtown members that didn't get released right away backed me up and I backed them up in conflicts with other losers who wanted to hog the two phones or one TV we all had to share.

Those three awful days while the reality of what had happened kept burning into my soul, dragging me ever lower, were just the beginning of my life going to hell in a hand basket. The downward path I'd started on by deciding to party one last time would only become more treacherous and steep in the coming years.

Chapter 11

It seemed like it took the D. A. just about forever to prosecute my case. After three days in the fish tank, I was arraigned and charged with first-degree murder. The judge asked me whether I wanted a trial by jury, but I said no, I'd rather just have my case presented to him and let him decide my fate.

That was supposed to speed things up so I could get on with serving my prison sentence.

But there turned out to be no way to hurry my case along.

I kept being shuffled from one county institution to another for the next seven months while the police handling my case kept asking for delays. It seems the Highland Park station was being moved into a new building, and somewhere along the way they lost the evidence against me.

Instead of giving up on prosecuting the case, they kept asking for extensions and getting them.

And all that time I lived in mortal fear for my life.

Up till then I'd always been the enforcer of gang laws.

Now I found myself on the other side of that merciless justice system. Ever since I was a small boy, I'd realized on some level that who lived and died, who got rich, and who got maimed, was decided by higher powers, out there somewhere. And everything I'd done to prove how tough and ruthless I was had been done to prove that I was worthy of being affiliated with that higher power. We called the people who ran the neighborhood gangs The Organization.

I'd known for many years that some members of Mike's family were closely connected—affiliated with The Organization. Not his father and mother, but others.

One day when I was just eight years old, I overheard Playboy, Mike's older brother (uncle, actually), talking about how a particular person was going to get hurt. Then, when I was still just eight, I witnessed a murder for the first time. The very man that Playboy had said was going to be hurt was stabbed to death as I looked on from a distance.

As horrible as that was for me, it delivered a message. Playboy had connections with the higher powers. The reason he was able to buy and sell heroin in large quantities in Mike's dad's workshop was that he was part of the over-the-top violent Organization. He had protection and connections.

What made that bad for me is that now the word on the street was that I had killed an Organization member's brother.

What hope did I have of not being greenlighted?

Once you've been greenlighted, you have a target painted on your back, and any Organization minion who has a chance to kill you is responsible to do so. If he doesn't, then he'll be greenlighted too and soon end up dead.

As I was shuffled from one jail to another, I could feel that target painted on my back. I knew I had to be looking over my shoulder all the time, and that I didn't dare get too close to anyone. A chief strategy of The Organization is to give your closest friend the job of killing you. If he refuses, he knows his own days are numbered.

In order to deflect the anger focused on me, I just kept putting in work, with a lot of effort, for The Organization.

Only by doing that could I try to maintain a balance and keep them in some small way on my side. If they needed me to do things for them—anything at all—then they'd keep me around. Maybe.

I have tried to forget the things I did for them. I don't want to bring up those memories now.

With hindsight I can see that it was only by the grace of God that I lived through those months in county custody, often in dormitory-type cells where night stabbings are as contagious as the common cold. At the time I attributed my survival to my own street smarts and willingness to do whatever it took to make myself valuable to the warlords who dictated where and when violent work could be done. Only the experience of later years has helped me realize that even doing good work for that group is no guarantee of another day of life.

Finally, after seven months of delays, I had my day in court. In April, 1984, the judge sentenced me to serve five years in state prison.

My first stop was the California Institution for Men in Chino, just east of Los Angeles in San Bernardino County. This huge prison serves as a reception center for prisoners. You're usually housed there for a short time while the powers-that-be decide where to send you for longer-term incarceration.

This was my first time in state custody, so despite my long rap sheet and reputation as a street hoodlum,

Edmundo Ramirez

someone must have thought that maybe there was
something redeemable in my soul, if I'd just make
some new associations and maybe learn some new
skills. At least I have to assume that's why they
decided to send me to the Sierra Conservation Center
(SCC), a low-to-medium security facility west of
Yosemite National Park. In that facility inmates are
trained in firefighting techniques, then sent to
unwalled conservation camps throughout the state to
be on call to fight forest fires and serve in other types
of emergencies.

Why didn't I take advantage of that opportunity,
you might wonder. Take that as my chance to leave my
violent past behind. Make new friends among the less-
violent inmates, take advantage of the wide variety of
vocational training programs on the campus.

That would have been the smart thing to do, but I
wasn't very smart, I guess. I wasn't really ready to
settle down and live an ordinary life, no matter how
much I had dreamed of it before Mike got shot.

Instead of trying to learn how to live as a law-
abiding citizen, I used my time stirring up trouble at
SCC.

The last straw came when I decided that the
Mexican-American prisoners ought to wrest control of
the TV room from the black prisoners who had been
changing the channels and enforcing their will.

I organized my compadres into a fighting unit that
managed to drive our opponents out of the room, but
in the process got myself driven out of that low-
security institution and sent to Soledad Prison.

Chapter 12

I'm not a fast learner, I guess you could say. At least not when it comes to learning how to behave in a civilized way.

But my activities at Soledad did earn me what The Organization considers a promotion. When I first got there, I kept to myself, wouldn't even sit at a table to eat with anyone else if I could help it. But finally a guy who I knew had affiliations invited me into his group. For some reason I came to trust him, and he was honorable enough to keep a watch on my back.

With his backing, and with my confidence growing, I began to assert myself more and more violently. My cellmate had been trying to dominate me, threatening to keep some of my things if I ever got transferred. Finally I got tired of it and beat him up pretty bad.

That earned me a transfer to an institution that, to the criminal mind, is something like getting accepted to Stanford University. That institution is Folsom Prison, one of the hardest of the hard-time prisons in the nation. It's the prison Johnny Cash once performed in, and it is of course the subject of one of his most famous songs, "Folsom Prison Blues."

Edmundo Ramirez

Most of my time in Folsom was spent in lockdown. I lived alone in a cell all but 1½ hours a day, and was only allowed to go out to the prison yard for an hour three times per week. Part of the time my cell was on the fifth tier, where I could look out at the other inmates strolling about and exercising in the yard.

More times than I like to remember, I also saw prison justice meted out by members of one of the four gangs that control all of California's prisons. Justice usually took the form of stabbings, when a man least expected it—when he wasn't watching his back.

According to a report released by the California Joint Legislative Committee on Prison Construction and Operations, 1985 was the most violent year in Folsom up to that time. In the first five months there were 120 stabbings, two of them fatal. [1] It was at this time, according to inmate accounts, that gang leaders were tacitly given a free hand to try to bring things under control by "cleaning up" their own members. Many of the stabbings were between rival gangs, but others were carried out between members of the same gang as gang heads tried to "take out the trash."

During the times I wasn't locked down, I kept doing my best to prove my value to the people at the top of The Organization by doing their bidding.

When I paroled out of Folsom on October 11, 1986, exactly three years and one month after Mike got shot, I guess you could compare it to graduating from college cum laude. I now had a "degree" behind my

---

[1] Joint Legislative Committee on Prison Construction and Operations, "California's Prisons: Violence at Folsom Prison: Causes, Possible Solutions" (1985). *California Joint Committees.* Paper 60, front matter.
http://digitalcommons.law.ggu.edu/caldocs_joint_committees/60

name, earned at one of the toughest institutions of higher learning in the criminal world.

If you didn't grow up in the kind of neighborhood I did, it may be difficult for you to understand what I mean by that, but kids on my block grew up listening to the big, tough men we admired talk about doing hard time, and how it hardened them and taught them how to get ahead in life. Guys they'd done time with were like fraternity brothers to them. Prison for them had been like a college experience, living in an especially-tough frat house. A Folsom tat is something like a Phi Beta Kappa pin, I guess you could say.

Maybe you grew up admiring a great preacher or musician or teacher, but kids in our neighborhood grew up admiring street toughs. The message we heard over and over again is that you're not really tough till you've been to prison. The word Folsom was spoken almost reverentially. Guys who'd been there knew what life was really all about.

That was before the term Pelican Bay had entered our vocabulary. The hardest-of-the-hard-time prisons in California was still under construction in 1986. In 1989 I would have the "privilege" of being one of the first inmates to move into Pelican Bay, the one prison with a population even more hardcore than Folsom, because the lessons I learned in Folsom were not what the justice system would have wanted me to learn; in fact they were just the opposite.

What I'd learned there was that the only way to stay safe in my world was to be tougher, meaner, more ruthless than anybody else around, and to execute orders received from the higher power that controlled our neighborhood immediately and without question.

That was what I was doing when I had Stretch shot a couple years later, in 1989.

But he was far from the first victim of my do-whatever-it-takes attitude.

I hit the streets running when I got out of Folsom in 1986. There was a major turf war going on at the time, and my gang brothers were glad to press me back into service doing enforcement. Anybody who failed to carry out an order, anybody who backed away from doing an assigned hit, anybody who tried skimming some money or drugs from their assigned sales territory, and especially anybody from a rival gang who tried to intrude on Avenues' turf could expect a visit from Bullet. And if they survived my visit, they'd have experienced enough pain to teach them not to try it again.

I'm not proud of the things I did. In fact I wish I could forget them, and that's why I'm not going to rehearse them here.

What my official criminal record shows is that my Christmas present in 1986, less than three months after parole, was a trip back to the California Institution for Men in Chino on December 24 for violating my parole. I was ordered to finish my original term, which would mean another 23 months in prison.

Of course in the prison system, you can usually get out early for good behavior, or simply because there's no room for you anymore, so it wasn't long till I was on the streets again, violating my parole. By the end of August, 1987 I was back in prison again, because as a felon I'd gotten caught in possession of a firearm (no big surprise there), which is a violation of parole.

This time they sent me to Avenal State Prison, and

because it had finally sunk in with them that I was a pretty incorrigible trouble-making street hoodlum, I spent the rest of 1987 and much of 1988 in solitary confinement there, finishing most of the rest of the five-year sentence that had begun in September, 1983 after Cholo Mike was killed.

Had my hard time in prison taught me my lesson?

Not the lesson the state wanted me to learn.

Back on the street to me meant back in business—gang business, that is. My assignment was to collect "taxes" from a whole cadre of drug pushers and send $5,000 a week to gang members back in the prison.

Soon, though, events began coming together in a way that would finally teach me what I really needed to know about life.

Chapter 13

We're to Chapter 13 now, and if you can still remember how I started this story, you'll recall that I was in church. How and why did I get there? I hope you're still wondering. Don't worry, we're getting close to finding out.

Remember my friend Pete, whose street name was Fat Boy? The guy who got shot in my car back in 1980?

Well, we'd had a few encounters in the intervening years. When I was still in county jail in 1983, waiting for my court date, Pete and another good friend were processed through there on a charge of armed robbery. Having only one good arm didn't stop Pete from strong-arming people.

But then, after he beat that charge and got out of jail, Pete had a conversion experience. It wasn't something he was looking for, but one day Nancy Chavez, whom we called Smiley, invited him to go to church with her. It didn't interest him in the least, but later that day, as he tells it, "I was wandering the streets, on my way to score some dope, when I literally forgot where I was going, and I was walking down the street, past Mundo's house, saying Where was I going? What was I gonna do? And I felt a tugging like something was tugging at me, pulling me. And I remember walking real fast and getting scared like, oh man, I'm losing it. And I remember getting to this house, knocking on the door."

A girl from the Dogtown gang came to the door. "Is Smiley here?" Pete asked.

"Yeah, what's happening Fat Boy?"

"I wanna go to church."

Of course Smiley was glad to take him.

That night in church he felt like the preacher was talking directly to him, like the guy totally understood everything about him, knew where he'd been, what he'd done, and probably what he was going to do next.

The message hit him right between the eyes, and he says that when there was an altar call at the end, he almost ran to the front. He realized how badly he had hurt his family, and he suddenly knew he wanted to change. In tears he repented of his wayward life and asked Jesus to come into his heart and change him. "I can't do it on my own, I can't," he admitted, and that day he became a Christian. He didn't suddenly change into a do-gooder with no bad habits, but that started him down the path to a crime-free life.

When I found out about that, it didn't make me happy at all.

I think I was in Soledad at the time, and I always looked forward to when the mail cart would come around, because Pete would write to me fairly often, and in the letters he'd talk about how I'd be getting out soon, and how he was lining up some fine-looking ladies for us to party with.

Then all of a sudden his letters changed, and he started dishing out all the stuff he'd been learning in church about love and forgiveness and learning to live a righteous life, and it didn't interest me in the slightest. A lot of times I'd just toss his letters on the table in my cell without even opening them.

All my life I'd believed religion was only for the weak; where I lived, you had to be strong. I didn't appreciate him preaching to me.

Then, while I was in Folsom in 1985, something really remarkable happened to Pete. There was a big evangelistic campaign down in Anaheim, and Smiley took him with her to one of the meetings.

At the end of the meeting there was another altar call, but this time the preacher wanted anybody who felt the need of healing in their life to come down to the altar for special prayer.

Well, as you can imagine, a guy with a paralyzed arm, with an irremovable bullet still lodged by his elbow, did feel the need of healing. But he was seated way up in the balcony, his right arm curled into his chest "like a chicken leg" as he described it.

Hearing the appeal to come to the front for healing, Pete considered it, but leaned over to Smiley and said, "If God can really heal people, I don't think I have to go all the way down there. If God's real, and he can really heal people, then he can touch me right here."

There was music playing and people praying, and a lot of people were going down to the altar. Pete says, "I remember lifting up my left arm and saying in my mind, 'God heal me. If you're real, and you do heal people, then heal me.' And all of a sudden I became aware that I had raised my right arm in the air too. I didn't even notice it right away, but there it was up in the air like my left arm!"

Before that he hadn't been able to lift the arm or use his hand. From that day forward to this day thirty years later, he has almost perfect use of the right arm and hand.

When I heard about that, it made an impression on me. It at least made me think that maybe there is a god who cares about people.

But I still didn't want anything to do with God or religion. I didn't think I needed it. The only higher power I was interested in pleasing was the power of the gang leaders who called the shots in my world.

I visited Pete once while I was out on parole in 1987. By that time he'd gotten married and had a little daughter, Ruby, and he was pastoring a small church congregation in San Gabriel. It was nice to see him, but the looks I got from his wife Nellie and his mother-in-law Mary Garcia let me know I better not come around too often. Mary Garcia had this way of looking at you that showed a lot of wisdom, and that she wasn't going to take any nonsense from you. Those two women didn't want me tempting Pete back into his old ways, so they were going to keep an eye on me.

For my part, I didn't feel at all tempted to join him in his new ways.

Chapter 14

My world and my ways all continued to revolve around the life of a street thug working his way up in The Organization, earning a reputation and respect by being the meanest *vato* on the block.

And my reputation worked for me.

There was a guy who was powerful in The Organization, who I'll call Big T.

I looked up to Big T, and he was also a good friend—at least I thought of him as one at that time. You'll hear more about him later.

While I was out of prison in 1989, after finishing serving my time for parole violation, Big T was in prison, and he asked a favor of me. It seems his parents were managing an apartment building, and they had a problem tenant. This guy would have big parties and play loud music all hours of the night. They'd gone to him repeatedly, even called the police on him, but he didn't care. The problem continued.

His folks came by, along with his younger brother, Little T (Lil T) and asked if I'd do them the favor of talking to their problem tenant.

I was glad to do it for a friend, especially one with

the high level of affiliation that Big T had. Let's just say that after I talked to the guy, Big T's parents didn't have any more trouble with him. I attributed that to the reputation I had on the street. The guy didn't fear the police, he didn't fear the parents of even a top gang leader, but he did fear a person with my connections and my reputation. That made me feel good, and powerful.

It also made a big impression on Lil T. He was several years younger than me, and nowhere near as tough or as connected, except through his brother, and I didn't really want to associate with him. But I couldn't exactly tell him to get lost. That would be disrespecting Big T, which would probably get me killed. Really, in that society, insults are taken that seriously.

So we began to hang out together. I'd take him with me on enforcement jobs, show him the ropes. I was his teacher, training him how to be a good gangster while his brother was in prison. And that's how Stretch got back into the picture.

Nobody can really explain how the hierarchy of a street gang is organized. Where you fit on the totem pole can change from day to day, and where other people think you fit is pretty subjective.

Stretch had a lot of clout on the streets.

He's a big guy, and he was built like a gladiator. Handsome, strong, not the kind of guy you'd want to tangle with—unless you had a lot of backing.

Lil T understood that he should leave Stretch alone, but he didn't think the big guy would really give him any trouble, for fear of retribution from his big brother's friends.

By early spring 1989 Stretch, on the other hand, was getting pretty tired of Lil T showing him attitude about some things Stretch had done several years earlier.

What Stretch had done was move in on Big T's girlfriend, the mother of two of Big T's kids while Big T was in prison.

Since the kids were Lil T's nephews, he thought of the girlfriend as his sister-in-law, even though she'd never married Big T. All this had happened years ago, and Stretch was now married to another woman and had a family of his own, but Lil T kept getting in his face about old news.

Unfortunately for Stretch, he didn't seem to understand his place in the order of things. Or if he did understand it, he let his emotions get in the way of his better judgment.

It all came to a head one day in March in 57 Park.

Chapter 15

In Highland Park there's a city park called Arroyo Seco. It's right beside a concrete-sided river bed (arroyo) that's dry most of the time, but channels runoff into the Los Angeles River whenever there's a storm.

Neighborhood people call it 57 Park because it's near the end of Avenue 57, right where you can get directly onto the Pasadena Freeway, which follows the arroyo from Pasadena to downtown Los Angeles. Originally the highway was part of the famous Route 66, and it's also known as the world's first freeway, having been opened in 1940. It's now known as the Arroyo Seco Freeway, but in 1989 it was called the Pasadena Freeway.

Members of various sets of the Avenues Gang hang out in the park all the time, at least they did back in my day. It's a favorite gathering spot, not for planning the next hit or anything, just a place to hang out with your homeboys, drinking, doing whatever drugs are available, socializing, and tossing the occasional insult just to see what kind of reaction you'll get.

Lil T and I drove into the park to hang out that

afternoon, but trouble started as soon as Lil T spotted Stretch there. And it only got worse as Lil T started feeling his oats with a few beers under his belt.

He started harping on the past again, insulting Stretch, trying to get him mad.

And it was working.

I could see Stretch getting agitated. He'd had quite a bit to drink, too, and he was turning into an angry drunk.

"Just leave it alone, *chavala!*" he shouted at Lil T.

"Who you callin' *chavala?*" Lil T responded, moving in closer. *Chavala* is a word that's not used much these days, but it's probably the Mexican equivalent of calling someone a no-good punk.

"You, *chavala!*" Stretch leaned in on him.

Lil T was looking my way, and without saying anything I let my eyes warn him to back off. He gave Stretch a domineering smile, then turned away, strutting like a peacock.

"That punk. I'm gonna kill him," Stretch said under his breath, just loud enough for me to hear.

"Listen man, just swallow your pride. It's not worth it, Bro. You know he's got backup. You don't wanna go there."

"I could pound him into the ground with one hand tied."

"I know, I know, man. But you don't wanna go there. Just leave it alone. *Calma la,* homie. Be the big man. He's too young to know he ain't got the world on a string just because his brother's got connections."

"Somebody needs to teach him a lesson."

"I'm tryin'. He's a slow learner, but I'm tryin' homie. Just let it die. I'll try to get him outa here soon. Okay?"

"You better, or he's not leavin' in one piece."

"You don't wanna go there, Bro. You don't wanna go there!"

Stretch flicked his head to the side, glaring at Lil T, who'd stopped on the far side of the group and was eyeing us as we talked.

I thought I had everything under control, and I was just getting ready to drag Lil T away with me, when the kid had another fit of stubbornness and started hurling threats and insults at Stretch again.

Stretch had had enough. Enough to drink, and enough of the mouthing off. And the two got mixed together in his brain and completely overpowered his better judgment. "You wanna settle this once and for all?" he shouted at Lil T.

"Yeah, I do!"

Stretch motioned with his head toward a tunnel leading under Avenue 60 that divides the park into two halves.

Lil T knew what he meant.

The fight would be taken away from the crowd, where they would go at each other one-on-one.

"Are you crazy?" I shouted, grabbing Lil T by the arm. "Don't do it, man. He's twice your size and twice as good a fighter."

"For my brother," was all Lil T said, pulling away from me.

"Don't do it, Bro. Come on, let's split!"

All my warnings and pleading fell on deaf ears. Stretch turned and stalked toward the tunnel, and Lil T followed him. What happened in that isolated end of the park was painful to watch, especially for me. I considered both combatants my friend, and I knew that how ever the fight came out, there wouldn't be any real winner. Everybody was going to end up getting hurt and hurt bad, one way or the other.

By the time Stretch was done whaling on Lil T, the kid's face looked like it had been put through a grinder. That was the way Lil T got hurt bad. Stretch's time was yet to come, I knew.

But I don't think Stretch was sober enough to realize how much pain he had set himself up for.

I did, though. Because there was a meeting I knew I had to attend that night.

Chapter 16

I had no choice but to take Lil T with me to the meeting of gang leaders that night. Shot callers from various gangs met once a week or so, to discuss how things were going and give each other the heads up about any problems that might be coming along.

When the other gang leaders saw Lil T, they of course wanted to know what had happened and who had made mincemeat of his face, and he was all-too-happy to tell them, putting the full blame on Stretch of course.

The other guys looked at me, and I didn't dare contradict what Lil T had said. That would be chalked up as being disloyal to Big T, and to the higher power that controlled our gangs.

After the other gang leaders had conferred for just a few minutes, a Made Man—one of the true powerhouses in the gang structure—came to me. "You gotta take care of this, Bala," he said.

I nodded. But my heart was breaking. I've always had a lot of love for Stretch, and I knew exactly what was meant by "take care of this."

"Do it now, before he gets a chance to run."

I nodded again and motioned for Lil T and two other guys to follow me. The extra bodies would be for backup in case we ran into trouble.

My mind was running full speed, and by time we got to my car, I had a plan mapped out in my mind, and I shared it with Lil T, drawing a rough sketch of the park on a scrap of paper and explaining exactly what was going to go down. The other two got in their car and followed me as we headed toward 57 Park.

All the way there I was hoping Stretch had had enough sense to split right after the fight. I didn't want to hurt him. In grade school his little brother had been one of my closest buddies.

But friendship only goes so far when it comes to gang loyalty. Letting friendship stand in the way of carrying out a directive from above is like asking someone to put a knife or bullet through your heart.

By this time I'd had a lot of experience carrying out hits without getting caught, and I knew the area around the park really well, so it was easy for me to come up with what I thought was a foolproof plan for taking care of business and getting away.

I parked my car on Via Marisol, up a short hill and through some trees from where the gang was hanging out. From there we couldn't see what was going on below us, but we could hear music playing and a lot of chatter, so we knew the group was still there.

I reached under my seat and produced three guns. One was a .25 caliber automatic pistol, one was a .357, and the third was a .38. I handed the .38 to Lil T, then rehearsed our plan once again.

When we got out of the car I went back and talked to the guys who had parked behind us. "Wait here. If anybody follows us out of the park, light them up." I didn't mean turn the headlights on them, though. *Light them up* meant shoot to kill.

From the parking spot Lil T and I had to walk down Via Marisol to get to the park entrance. We could see some activity going on there, too, and as we got closer we realized that a C.R.A.S.H. unit must be planning a raid on the group in the park. There were three unmarked detective cars there and half-a-dozen cruisers. Twenty or thirty officers were gathered around one of the cars, as their leader laid out their next move.

What horrible timing! We were about to walk into the middle of a police gang-enforcement raid. What happened next probably reveals more about my mentality at that time than anything else I could tell you.

I mean, just think about it. I didn't really want to kill Stretch.

All the way there, I'd been hoping he'd had enough sense to be halfway to Nevada by the time Lil T and I came back looking for him.

Now I'm at the park, and I realize everybody there's about to be arrested anyhow. What a perfect excuse to just call it a night and tell the powers above me that I'd gone to the park to try to handle the situation, but the police were already there getting ready to arrest everybody, so it would have been stupid for me to get mixed up in that mess. If they wanted Stretch killed, there'd be plenty of chances for someone to off him at the jailhouse.

But did I welcome that potential excuse and turn tail? No. You know what Lil T and I did? We walked

Edmundo Ramirez

right by the army of lawmen preparing to raid the park, packing heat. If they'd happened to stop me for a routine check, I'd have been in handcuffs immediately, because I was a felon carrying two pistols concealed under my jacket.

What I'm saying is that at that point in my life, my loyalty to the gang, and the urgency I felt for advancing in the gang culture, overruled everything else in my life. This hit would earn me more stripes, and that mattered more than friendship or my own safety or anything else.

There's a big oak tree just past the park entrance, and seventy-five yards farther on the arroyo crosses under the road. With the tree shielding us from view, we hopped over the fence and down onto the concrete shoulder of the stream, which we could follow along the northwest edge of the park. We were less than fifty yards from the freeway, so we didn't have to worry much about making noise; our footsteps would be drowned out by traffic.

Three-hundred yards upstream, we hopped the fence again, behind some trees, and began moving stealthily toward the gathered gang.

To my dismay I could plainly see that Stretch was still there.

"You know what to do, then," I said to Lil T.

"You got it, Ese," he said. He was still enraged and humiliated by the beating he'd taken, and he had no compunctions about carrying out his mission.

"Be sure to reserve one bullet, in case they start to chase you."

"Right."

The magazine held six bullets.

I stood up from my crouch then, and walked toward the group.

On the far side of the gathering was a small building that housed restrooms, and there was a street light there.

It didn't take long for people to notice me, and soon every eye was on me.

I walked over and stood under the light, holding their attention, nodding my head in a way to show that I had everything under control. I'm sure everyone was on edge, wondering what I was about to do. Instinctively the crowd parted a bit, leaving room around Stretch, just in case lead started to fly.

With everyone's attention focused on me, Lil T walked up behind his target. "Hey, Stretch, I just wanted to be sure everything's cool, okay?" he said, catching the big guy by surprise.

As Stretch turned to face him, Lil T emptied all but one bullet into him, hitting him five times from point blank range.

The crowd erupted in screams.

Stretch crumpled to the ground, blood spurting from wounds in his chest, neck, jaw, shoulder, and back.

Taking advantage of the shock and surprise he'd caused, Lil T took off running up the hill toward the car. It took a couple seconds, but soon some of the gang leaders were hot on his tail, and others were heading my way.

I took off running, joining Lil T on the way up the hill. When it seemed like our pursuers might be gaining on us, I pulled out the .357 and turned around and fired one shot over their heads, making them all dive for the dirt. We weren't there to hurt anyone else, we were on a mission of vengeance against one man only.

It took us less than a minute to get to the car. We got in and calmly drove down the street past the gathered police operation, which of course had been disrupted by the sound of gunfire. The police all headed into the park, but by time they had closed off the crime scene, Lil T and I were cruising down the freeway.

You would think that someone who was there at the park would have put the finger on us, ratted us out, told the police who did the shooting. But if that's what you think happened, you haven't yet come to understand the gang mentality that rules that neighborhood.

You learn early on, living there, that snitches end up in ditches. There is no worse sin in that culture than cooperating with a police investigation. There is only one penalty for anyone who rats on another gang member. "Justice" may be swift, or it may lie in wait for an opportune moment. But there is no possibility of appeal.

So I walked away from that crime scot free. We soon learned that Stretch had survived the attempt on his life, but that didn't matter a whole lot. I'd carried out the mission I'd been given, and I'd gotten away with conspiracy to commit murder. I was untouchable!

But before long my luck would run out.

You can understand now, though, why it was with fear and trepidation that I took that seat directly in front of Stretch in church that Sunday morning eight years later. We hadn't spoken in the intervening years, hadn't even seen each other. I'd spent most of those years behind bars. But in that culture, time passing doesn't make a bit of difference. By all the standards of the gang culture in which Stretch and I had grown up, he was obligated to kill me on sight.

What remained to be seen was whether there was a power even higher than the gang culture operating in his life and mine by this time.

Chapter 17

You might think that the events of that March day would have traumatized me, made me stop and think over the course my life was following. After all, conspiring to attempt to murder a close friend is a pretty traumatic thing. But for me it was just another day's work in the service of the higher power that controlled my life.

Still, though, when you do something like that and walk away unscathed, it does something to your psyche. The more evil you get away with doing, the more you need to do to keep the adrenalin flowing and to silence any qualms that might start to trouble you.

My reputation now was way up there among the people on the street who knew what I had done, and I was strutting my stuff like never before.

The thing about power, though, is that the more you get, the more you want. So I was always looking for something more to do to make an impression. I'd take on any assignment, no questions asked.

A few weeks after we tried to assassinate Stretch, I was down on Verdugo Road, not far from where I'd gotten shot a few years earlier, and a guy in front of a liquor store started hurling insults at me. He was drunk, and so was I—not only drunk, but strung out on cocaine. If my better faculties had not been totally numb, I probably would have ignored him.

His better faculties were numb as well, and on top of that he was trying to impress his wife, who was with him. "Hey, you filthy cholo!" he yelled, playing the big man.

I wouldn't take that from anyone. I went over to him and got right in his face, my hands hanging at my sides, showing him I wasn't afraid of him. "What you calling me?"

He was too drunk to back down. "A filthy," and with that he spat on the sidewalk, "*cholo.* You think you're so tough. Well, I got news for you. I'm the only one that calls the shots around here." That's a sanitized version of what he said, using Spanish curse words.

My left fist instantly came around and caught him square on the jaw, knocking him flat.

He slowly picked himself up and backed up just a little, continuing to leer at me.

The correct exercise of power, as every gang enforcer knows, is to keep it under control. Don't let your emotions get the best of you. No matter how violent the job you have to carry out, do it while sober. Take long, slow breaths. Maintain total control of your body, your emotions, and of your environment as far as possible.

Hubris, on the other hand, is the enemy of self-control. Once you get a taste of absolute power, you begin to think the world revolves around you and you can command the sun to rise and set at will.

I'd walked away from the job in 57 Park unscathed,

and I'd begun to think I had the world on a string. Now, in my drunk and drugged state, I let my anger get the best of me.

The man wiped spittle from his lip that was starting to swell, and said under his breath, "Cholo," as he started to turn toward his car.

"I'm sorry, I didn't hear you. What did you call me?"

"A filthy cholo," he said, turning back to face me. His wife by now was screaming at him to just let it go and shut up, but he wasn't about to take orders from anyone.

This guy was defying me! I marched up and hit him again, and he went down on the ground. It was a real struggle for him to get up this time, but he managed, and was slinking toward his car when I hit him again.

Sprawled on his back, he managed to get up again, and I hit him again, knocking him back against his car. I began punching him over and over again, in a total blind rage, all my pent-up anger pouring out through my fists.

"Leave him alone!" his wife was screaming from behind me. Later, in court, she said I was pounding on him like an out-of-control kid with a rag doll.

Finally I stopped punching him long enough to turn around and smile at the woman.

She began making her way to him, and he turned and opened the door of his car to get in.

My rage wasn't fully spent yet, though, so I reached under my jacket to where, as usual, I had a small pistol concealed. I pulled it out, pointed it at the man, and pulled the trigger.

He slumped into his seat, and I turned, glared at his wife who was screaming at me, and walked calmly to my car, a '69 Chevy Nova, and drove the mile to my parents' house.

The new house we'd built on the property had a separate apartment in the basement that you got to from behind the house, and that's where I went. I took a shower, got something to eat, and lay down for a nap, totally unconcerned I guess, about what I had just done. Drugs and alcohol take a lot away from you. At this point they had completely removed any good sense I might have had, a point that will become obvious to you when you hear what I did next.

Chapter 18

When I woke up from my nap there in the basement apartment of my parents' house, I felt refreshed and ready for some more action. The police hadn't come knocking yet, so I figured they didn't know who had shot the guy.

Our gang had a hangout down by the liquor store where I'd shot the man just a few hours earlier, but I figured by now it was dark and all the commotion would have settled down, so I got in my car and drove down there to see what was going on.

As I pulled into the parking lot, though, I noticed a uniformed policeman staring at me. As soon as he saw me, he went for his gun and pointed it at me and ordered me to stop and get out of the car.

I floored it, burning rubber, and roared back onto the street, jamming the headlight knob forward, shutting off all my lights as I did.

The officer jumped into his squad car and took off after me. I led him on a bit of a chase through the winding hills, and even managed to shake him a couple times, but he always spotted me again.

When I got to the street by my parents' house, my

Edmundo Ramirez

plan was to continue past the end of the pavement and down a dirt road into a nearby park, but somebody had left their car in the way, blocking the entrance to the dirt road, so I slowed down, opened the door, and rolled out onto the ground.

My car kept on going, and plummeted down the side of the hill into the sage brush and black walnut trees growing there. I heard a loud bang when it ran into a tree, but I didn't take time to look and see what had happened. I was going full speed around to the back of my parents' house. It was dark, though, and I must have stepped in a hole or something, because I turned my right ankle, spraining it real bad.

When I picked myself up off the ground, I was in excruciating pain and could barely walk, but I made it down the hill and into the basement apartment whose door was on the rear of the house.

The policeman didn't see me bail out of the car, so he took off down the hill, pointing his pistol at my car and ordering me to get out. Which, of course, didn't pan out for him.

Soon there were squad cars all up and down our street, and they were using a megaphone to order everyone to come out of the house.

A bunch of my little nephews and nieces were upstairs with their parents, and nobody up there had any clue what was going on. They hadn't heard me come into the downstairs apartment.

The police ordered everybody out of the house, and these little kids ended up standing around, getting chilled, until some kind neighbors offered to let them come into their houses.

The police searched the house and came up empty.

There was a huge walnut tree covering most of the back yard, and they didn't look around carefully enough at first to figure out that there was another apartment downstairs.

At the time there had been several murders happening not far away in Griffith Park, so the police had a special taskforce operating in the area, and they all converged on the scene. Police cars all over the place and four helicopters hovering overhead, and I was just hunkering down there, all alone in the basement.

I had a lot of time to think. What to do? End it all, or go back to prison? Those were my only two choices.

Finally someone in one of the choppers noticed the back door, and I heard them call down to the police on the ground about it.

Next thing I knew, the canine unit was there, pounding on the door, ordering me to come out with my hands up.

Should I go out and surrender, or go out firing my gun and commit suicide by police? If I surrendered, I'd for sure be facing lots of long, hard years in prison. But then again, the big house by now seemed like home away from home for me. I'd be with my own kind there, and with the stripes and street cred I'd earned while away, I'd probably get some pretty good perks on the inside.

You might wonder what I mean by that, but what you've got to realize is that prisons are not run by the wardens and guards. They aren't really the ones in power. Sure they have the keys, and they can decide where you'll live, and how long you'll stay. But they don't run the yard; they don't really control the inmates' lives. The real power lies in the hands of the prisoners themselves, and there is a strict hierarchy of control. The more street cred you have, the more tats from tough prisons you wear, the worse your reputation for violence, the more power you have, and the more perks you get.

I was a career criminal by now, and I was being offered a scholarship to one of my profession's primo institutions of higher learning.

I put my hands above my head, hollered out the door that I didn't have a gun, and walked out into the yard, where I obediently lay down, face down on the ground. Now it was the policemen's turn to vent all their pent-up anger, and they beat and kicked me while in the process of putting my new set of bracelets on. It was so bad that little children watching from next door began to scream at them to stop hitting me.

My sister, who saw them walk me away, said I was covered with blood.

I didn't really care, though. They asked me if I wanted to go to the hospital or to jail, and I chose to go directly to jail, refusing any medical treatment, even though in addition to the injuries I had received in the beating, my ankle was badly swollen, and I could barely hobble.

Chapter 19

By time I made it through county jail and the courts, and on into the state prison system, my reputation had preceded me, and word came down from the people in charge of the prison I was sent to that I was to be the one to run the yard I was assigned to. By that I mean, I was in charge of gathering up like-minded gang members and starting to enforce The Organization's will on the prisoners who spent part of the day out on the yard with me.

That meant that from time to time I'd get assignments to deal with someone who had been greenlighted for punishment, and I'd also collect "taxes" from gangs that our Organization dominated. About two months later, word came down to me, from an Organization leader that I respected, that my cellmate had been greenlighted.

Fortunately for me, unfortunately for him, I knew that the man in the cell next to ours was an expert at making shanks from pieces of scrap metal, so I passed a message to him in prison code. "Hey, I need to send a letter to someone, so would you draw a picture on an envelope for me?"

He knew exactly what I meant, and went to work right away. Word went up and down the cellblock, and other prisoners started beating out a rhythm with their hands to drown out the sound of a knife being sharpened on the concrete floor.

That evening he told me he had the envelope for me, so I went to the corner of the cell nearest him, and he passed me an envelope with a picture drawn on it. Inside was a sharpened piece of steel.

My cellmate said, "Hey, can I see the picture?"

"Sure, here's the picture," I said, handing him the envelope with my left hand and jabbing the 3-inch blade into his belly with my right hand in a single movement.

He screamed, of course, and the guards soon came running, but I managed to stab him several more times before they pulled me off him.

In a rush to get him to the infirmary, the guards carried him away and left me locked in the cell. By time they came back for me, I had cleaned up all the blood and flushed the shank down the toilet. Later the case would be dismissed for lack of evidence.

That attack, though, got me transferred to a tougher area of the prison, known as Palm Hall. It was the place they put guys who were regarded as hardened criminals and members of various gangs.

When I got there, I could see immediately that I had earned new respect and status by quickly carrying out the orders coming down from the higher power that controlled the prison. In fact, I had achieved what every gangster dreams of. I was a Made Man. Part of the elite, controlling cadre at the top level of The Organization.

What that meant was that now I was a shot caller. I could give the orders about who was to be greenlighted, who was to get special privileges, and how things would run. At that level, there is supposedly no hierarchy. Every Made Man is supposed to be regarded as an equal, but in reality some get more respect and control more territory than others. But there was no longer any boss I had to answer to.

I was walking on air. This is what I had striven all my life to achieve, ever since that first fight in the basement of Glassell Elementary. I was now a top dog, and nobody could tell me what to do.

The list of Made Men in The Organization is a tightly-guarded secret, but apparently the prison authorities had my number, because before long they gave me a scholarship to the highest of all institutions of higher learning in the California prison system: Pelican Bay.

I'd gained tremendous street cred by doing time in Folsom, but now a prison with even higher security had been constructed up in northern California, far away from the street gangs of the Los Angeles and San Francisco metropolitan areas.

The idea was that if gang leaders could be isolated and kept away from the cities, they would no longer be able to control things on the streets, which is what they had been doing from all the other prisons.

It seemed like a good idea, but it has never really worked. Prisoners have a lot of time on their hands, and they will figure a way around almost any restrictions the authorities try to impose.

It was a tremendous honor for me, one of the newest Made Men in The Organization, to be shipped

out on one of the first busses headed for Pelican Bay—
the place that would soon have a reputation as the
roughest prison in California.

I knew that now, with my hard-earned status in the
gang hierarchy, my time even in one of the hardest of
hard-time prisons in the nation would be a piece of
cake. Surely The Organization I had worked so
diligently for would see to it that I was treated well,
given special privileges, and generally made to feel
welcome and cared for there.

Surely ...

Chapter 20

Pelican Bay was and is the highest of all the higher-criminal-education prisons in the state of California, the state with more prisoners than any other.

And boy did I get educated there.

In the short time between becoming a Made Man and my transfer, I had begun to see cracks in the façade of The Organization.

I had begun to hear conflicting orders passed around.

That's a natural state of affairs, I realize now, in any outfit that claims everyone at the top level is equal. I've heard it said that in the Soviet Union the word was that all the comrades were equal, just some were a little more equal than others.

Any organization made up of people is going to have conflict. There will always be people claiming more rights than are due them, and others who are out to deny them those rights, or to claim them for themselves.

The myth that The Organization was a united front held true only in limited ways.

And the myth that The Organization takes care of

its own also turned out to be nothing more than a myth.

When I arrived at Pelican Bay, I was assigned a cell in the SHU. These excerpts from a Wikipedia article will help you understand the significance of that:

Pelican Bay State Prison (PBSP) is a supermax California Department of Corrections and Rehabilitation state prison in Crescent City, California. The 275-acre (111 ha) facility has an 'X' section designed to keep California's known "worst of the worst" prisoners in long-term solitary confinement. . . .

Pelican Bay opened in 1989. Pelican Bay's grounds and operations are physically divided. Half of the prison holds Level IV prisoners in a "general population" environment with outside exercise courts. The other half of the prison contains Pelican Bay's best-known feature: an X-shaped cluster of white buildings and barren ground known as the Security Housing Unit (SHU). . . .

The 8-by-10-foot (2.4 m × 3.0 m) cells of the Pelican Bay SHU, or Secure Housing Unit, are made of smooth, poured concrete. They have no windows. Instead, there are fluorescent lights, which the inmates can control. For at least twenty-two hours every day, prisoners remain in their cells, looking out through a perforated steel door at a solid concrete wall. Food is delivered twice a day (breakfast, sack lunch, and dinner) through a slot in the cell door.

A correctional officer in a central control booth controls these doors; he can press a button and allow one prisoner at a time to go out to a shower, or to his court-mandated five hours per week of outdoor exercise. This exercise takes place in a cement yard, often called a "dog run", which extends the length of three cells, and has a roof partially open to the sky. The correctional officer in the control booth is always armed; from his central vantage point in the control booth, he can shoot onto any one of six pods, each containing eight cells.

Being placed directly into the SHU as one of its first residents ought to have netted me a huge status boost. Who else in the whole Organization could claim that sort of cred?

That's the way I thought, anyhow.

But I was about to get a higher education in a subject I hadn't had the chance to study before.

During my first year in the Pelican Bay SHU, I had a lot of time to think, and a lot of questions that didn't seem to have good answers started to bother me.

All my life, from the time I was in grade school, I had poured myself into serving a group of people—an Organization that had real status in my world. Essentially I had spent my whole life climbing the corporate ladder of The Organization. Now, finally I was at the top. I had achieved the goal I had worked for, risked my life for, even killed for. So, where was the corner office on the top floor that I had dreamed of?

You get the picture, don't you? It's not that I expected to be given a cell with picture windows looking out over the Pacific Ocean three miles to the west, or into Jedediah Smith Redwoods State Park, just two-and-a-half miles to the southeast.

But as a Made Man, I expected that my comrades would see to it that I was at least comfortable in my solitary confinement cell. There are all kinds of perks available to prisoners with the right connections. A TV in your cell, for instance; decent toiletries from the commissary, snacks and good coffee from the canteen.

But you've got to have the right connections and be at the right spot in the power structure to get these things. Up till now, I'd always had those things provided to me, or I'd been able to strong-arm my way into getting them.

Now, sitting alone in my cell in the highest-security area of one of the highest-security prisons in the world, I had nothing. Not a single privilege to acknowledge my status in The Organization.

All I had was books, and a New Testament to read. No TV, no decent toiletries, nothing but state-issued stuff that was purchased from the lowest-price, and lowest-quality, suppliers the corrections department could find.

Had I spent my whole life pursuing nothing but a promise—a promise that would never be fulfilled?

Why was it that, after a lifetime of serving The Organization, following every directive to the letter, I was now one of their forgotten warriors?

After months with no meaningful contact, I began to realize that nobody in The Organization really cared about me or what happened to me or what I had done for them in the past. I was of very little use to them in my isolation cell. My role for them had always been Enforcer, and there wasn't much I could do in that line when I couldn't get close enough to anyone else to touch them, let alone stab them.

If The Organization had wanted to contact me or help me in any way, they easily could have, because communication systems were quickly set up within the SHU that allowed gang leaders to pass orders among inmates and to the outside world quickly, despite the state's best efforts to isolate us.

To make matters worse, I knew that my old homie Big T, the man for whom I had orchestrated the hit on Stretch, was also confined in the SHU, but for months he made no effort to contact me.

After I'd been there all alone for about a year, word began to filter down from the guards that some cells were going to have to double up. Finally I heard from Big T, telling me to request him as a cellmate, and saying that he would request me. After the requests were reviewed, we got approval. Don't ask me how—it seems like the authorities would have been aware that we were long-time gang associates, and they'd have never wanted us to be together. The whole idea behind building the Pelican Bay prison was to isolate gang members and keep them from communicating.

Be that as it may, Big T finally moved in with me after about a year, bringing his personal TV with him. By a strange coincidence I received the gift of a TV of my own the same day, from a childhood friend—a fellow-prisoner who I had helped out by doing some research in the law library for him.

The fact that I met another childhood friend there in that supermax prison gives you a picture of the kind of influences kids in my neighborhood had while they were growing up, doesn't it? Whatever prison I was in, I usually met some guys that I had grown up with.

Things were cool between Big T and me for a short while, but soon I began to realize he wasn't my friend at all. He still considered himself my superior, and anything and everything that went on in our cell had to circulate around him and be approved by him.

It wasn't long before I started to chafe against his domineering attitude.

In the couple years I'd been out of jail before shooting the drunk, I'd collected a lot of taxes for the gang, and had sent thousands of dollars into the prisons for the Brothers. In fact I'd sent thousands directly to Big T. Now he wouldn't share anything with me. Any money that came was his and his alone, and when he'd get something from the canteen, he'd never think of sharing it or asking if I wanted something too.

It was becoming clearer and clearer to me day by day that the supposed Brotherhood of leaders of The Organization was no such thing. Each and every one of the Brothers was looking out for himself and his family, and screw the rest. In fact there were severe jealousies and rivalries among the leaders.

I'd known for a long time that there was no love lost between Big T and one of my cousins, who was also one of the Brothers. So when Big T started to insinuate that The Organization was calling for a hit against my cousin, and implying that I was the one who was to carry it out as soon as I got out of prison, that put my antennae up even more. There was no reason my cousin should be greenlighted, except that Big T didn't like him.

Next I heard that my little brother Ernie had been greenlighted!

"What? Why?"

"Well, you know what happened the night Lil T shot Stretch, don't you?" Big T asked.

"What?"

"That guy that started shouting your name, saying 'Mundo, Mundo! It's Mundo! Get him!'"

"Yeah, what about him?"

"Well, somebody was supposed to take care of that rat for you."

"Yeah, did they?"

"That guy put the job off on Ernie. And he never did a thing. That's why he's greenlighted, and that's why it's your job to take care of him when you get out."

"You want me to kill my own brother and my cousin."

"That's the orders. You got a problem with that?"

I didn't say anything, just stretched out on my bunk, staring at the wall.

So, this is what it had come to. This is what it meant to be one of the Brothers. It didn't give you power, it just gave you trouble.

In fact I'd begun to notice that things had gotten worse for me in several ways since I achieved my supposedly-privileged status. Before that I was able to get away with all kinds of things. Once I was in, though, it seemed like the guards knew what I was going to do even before I did it. I was pretty sure somebody who knew my business was ratting on me.

This whole brotherhood and higher power thing wasn't working out for me at all.

But did I dare renounce my membership? *Blood in blood out* is the inviolable rule of gang membership. You shed blood to get in; if you want out, it will be your blood—all of it—that will be shed.

Chapter 21

I lay on my bed for a long time, thinking. If I refused Big T's order, I'd soon be dead. He was my cellmate, and he could easily see to that. What were my options? I didn't have any, really.

"So you got a problem with that *camarada?*" Big T said the next day, staring at me through hostile eyes.

"No. No problem," I said, returning his cold stare.

"Good," he said, fingering his neck in a way that I knew meant that if I did have a problem, it would be my neck on the chopping block next.

From that day forward I started resisting and antagonizing Big T in every way I could. It didn't take long to achieve my goal—getting away from him. When the fights got violent enough, I was moved to a different pod. Just before I left his cell, I told him I wasn't going to do what he'd ordered me to do, and that I was no longer taking any orders from The Organization.

He just smiled a knowing smile. Didn't say a word. He knew that I knew what that meant. That in that instant I had gone from being a Made Man to being a Marked Man. A green light was flashing on my back.

Once I moved out of Big T's cell, I felt I could breathe a little easier. At least I could go to sleep at night without worrying about waking up with a knife in my back.

But the battle wasn't over, not by a long ways. If the higher power I had served all my life didn't have me killed, it would be a sign of weakness on their part, which could lead to more rebellion in the ranks. I would have to watch my back very, very carefully, no matter where I went from here on out.

I paroled out of Pelican Bay in 1992, and immediately went to work pushing drugs. While I was hanging out in front of my house one day, a fellow called Bobby, who I knew as a top-notch house burglar, drove up in his pickup. "Hey man, what's happenin'?" he said through the open window.

"Not much."

"Come on, get in with me."

I looked him over cautiously. In gang life, when you know there's a target on your back, you have to watch your friends even closer than your enemies. It's standard protocol to assign a hit to the person who can get closest to the target without arousing suspicion. So I was suspicious of everybody.

I approached the truck slowly, watching for any sudden moves, my hand just millimeters from the little Saturday Night Special pistol I had tucked into my waistband.

There was a .38 automatic on the console.

He saw me looking at it.

"Come on, get in man, we're cool."

I opened the door and sat down without taking my eyes off the gun.

He had some beer with him, so we chugged a few cans, and when we were feeling mellow he said, "Yeah, I'm supposed to be killing you today."

"I figured."

There was a long silence.

"So, do what you gotta do, Bro," I said. "If that's what you came for." I figured if he was going to carry through, I could beat him to the gun that still lay on the console between us. Only one of us would get out of the truck alive, and I planned on it being me.

Bobby moved uneasily in his seat, his left arm out the window. He knew what was going through my mind.

I never took my eyes off the gun. If his right hand so much as twitched toward it, he'd be a dead man.

Finally he turned and looked out the window to his left. "Nah man, I ain't gonna do it."

"They'll greenlight you if you don't. Come on, let's get it over with."

"Nah man, I ain't got nothin' against you, Bro."

After that, Bobby never threatened me again. In fact, we began hanging out and getting high together. Eventually I came to have a certain amount of trust for him, but I always kept a wary eye on him after that.

There came a time when my drug business dried up because I didn't handle money very well. I didn't have enough cash to keep my "inventory" up, so I asked Bobby to teach me the burglary business.

He was a real expert, knew just where people usually stashed their small, easily-transportable, and easily-sold valuables. We could be into and out of a house in minutes without leaving a trace.

We carried on a successful partnership for several

months, then one night when he was pulling a job on his own, he got caught.

That was a bad break for me, I figured, because even though I'd been learning the tricks of the trade from him, I was nowhere near as good without him.

Funny thing was, though, that he went through county jail like it was a turnstile. He was back on the streets, and we were back in business six days later. Why didn't I ever catch a break like that?

In hindsight, maybe I should have been a little more suspicious about what had gone down while he was in police custody.

The following week we set out to look for an easy mark up in the hills above Azusa. Something didn't feel right about it, though. We were going out in broad daylight, which wasn't unusual for us, but some sixth sense was nagging at me. I almost told him to turn around and skip it for the day, but I didn't.

We drove just a little ways up into a canyon, but Bobby said it didn't feel right. I had to agree with him, so we went back down into Azusa and drove around for a while. Finally he spotted a house he said he had a feeling was a good one.

"You kidding me, man? The police station's just down the block!" I said.

"When's that ever been a problem for pros like us?" he smiled at me as he pulled his truck to a stop beside the curb and got out.

Within sixty seconds he'd found an unlocked window and crawled through it. Thirty seconds later he was opening the front door for me.

About two minutes later I heard a helicopter hovering overhead, and then an amplified voice from in front of the house said "We've got you surrounded. Come out with your hands up!"

I spent the next five months back at my home-away-from-home in the county jail, then it was off to prison, this time with a seven-year sentence.

The only way I got off that easy was that when I went to court four months later, I met an attorney who I knew claimed to be a Christian and begged him—if he really was a Christian—to go tell the judge I'd plead to whatever he wanted me to plead to, if he'd sentence me to just seven years. With a record like mine, I was looking at doing some serious years in the system this time around. If I couldn't cop a plea deal, I'd probably be locked up till I was ready to start collecting Social Security.

It wasn't easy to convince the attorney to represent me. When he asked me if I was a Christian, I was up front with him and told him that in fact I hated Christians, because I figured religion was only for the weak, and I figured a lot of guys in prison got religion just long enough to get early parole. That didn't sit well with him, but I kept appealing to his Christian mercy.

Truthfully, I was just working the system. I'd been exposed to Christianity enough to know that it was supposed to make people kind, merciful, and loving, so I figured I could use the guy's religion to my advantage. Let's face it, I was a con at heart, willing to con anybody, any way I could, to gain an advantage. Finally he caved in and went to the judge and managed to persuade him to give me that short sentence.

My troubles were far from over, though. For a man with a target painted on his back, prison is an even more dangerous place than the streets. I had survived so far by first depending on the higher power represented by The Organization, then by my own wits and bravado, keeping an eye out for enemies sent by that higher power.

In prison I would be faced with a choice of allegiances.

My life would depend on which side I chose.

Chapter 22

At the end of October, 1993, after spending more than four months in the county jail system, I was sent to North Kern State Prison to be evaluated for placement in a longer-term institution. A month after I arrived, I began to notice that one inmate in particular kept watching my every move, especially out in the exercise yard.

That, of course, made me suspicious. He must be the guy The Organization was telling to "take care of business" with me, so I kept a close eye on him. On the third of December, at the end of our exercise period, I was sure I saw a glint of sharpened steel in his hand as we were being herded back to our cells.

Rather than let him get behind me and stab me in the back, I charged at him and started hitting him.

Quickly an alarm sounded on the yard, and orders came through the public address for all prisoners to get down on the ground.

I wasn't about to turn my back on this guy, so I just kept hitting him, and of course he was hitting back as best he could. I'd caught him by surprise, and apparently he didn't have a shank in his hand, because he was fighting back with his fists.

The order came again "Get down on the ground!" and I ignored it again.

Then there was a loud bang, and a bullet from one of the guard towers whistled past my ear, missing my head by inches at the most.

That did it. I knew the guards had orders to shoot to kill. There was a no-warning-shot policy in force, and large signs around the yard constantly reminded us of that fact. So I grabbed my opponent by his jumpsuit and rolled him over my hip and slammed him down on the concrete, then backed off three steps and lay down, keeping my eyes on him. He had rolled over onto his stomach, and he was shaking like a leaf. I didn't feel too steady myself, after hearing that bullet buzz past me.

They tacked 90 days onto my sentence for that fight, but that was of little concern to me. I figured I'd delivered a message to anyone who might be watching me, much like I had done with Oso on the outside. They knew now that I wouldn't be going down without a fight.

I guess it must have been January 17, 1994 that I was transferred from North Kern State Prison to Centinela State Prison out in the desert, just a dozen miles from the Mexican border. The reason I know the date is that the prison bus had to detour around Los Angeles on the way to Centinela. At 4:30 that morning the Northridge Earthquake, one of the most powerful quakes ever to strike directly beneath an urban area, shook down freeway overpasses all over Los Angeles County.

Three weeks after I got to Centinela I was attacked by a group of inmates in the cafeteria. Once again there were no shanks or knives involved, fortunately, just a big kitchen spoon. This was the kind of fight I enjoyed, so again, even after the guards ordered us down on the ground, we kept going after each other, smashing our fists into each other's faces.

One of the guards came up behind me and tried to pull me down, but the other inmates kept coming at me, so I struggled, kicking at them. Finally, though, both the guard and I fell down, and I fell right on his leg, twisting his knee badly.

Later, in court, I could have had a lot of time added to my sentence for refusing his order to get down, but he was kind enough to testify that I'd actually done the right thing by continuing to fight, because if I'd lain down immediately, the others probably would have attacked him.

Once things settled down, that same guard escorted me back to my cell, limping heavily. Later another guard showed up at my cell to take me to the place they call The Hole—the Administrative Segregation Unit—solitary confinement. As he walked me to my new home, he began to talk to me about my life. "You know, Ramirez, what you need in your life?"

I didn't say anything.

"You need God in your life."

"Yeah, right. You sound like my mama. That's what she's always saying, but you know what, man? Religion is for cowards."

He just half-smiled and shrugged as he closed the door to my solitary cell.

As I looked around my new, stark surroundings, I knew I faced weeks of sheer frustration and boredom, like I had experienced in the SHU at Pelican Bay.

Edmundo Ramirez

"Hey man," I called out as the guard headed down the hall. "You got any books I can read?"

He came back, looked at me, and smiled. "Sure."

He went to a small closet and pulled out a Bible. "Here's a book you can read," he said as he laid it on the floor and kicked it under the bars to me.

What did I want with that book? Well, at least if I could get a little weed, I could use the pages to roll a joint. "Thanks, man," I said.

The book sat on a shelf, staring at me for days. Finally, out of sheer boredom, I decided to pick it up and start reading.

This wouldn't be the first time I had read portions of the Bible, not by a long shot. Up in Pelican Bay I'd had a New Testament, and I'd read it through over and over again—it seems like a hundred times.

But I didn't understand what I was reading. I was especially puzzled by texts that talked about blood being used to wash away sins, or to bring forgiveness. That made absolutely no sense to me. I had seen a lot of blood shed in my day. I had shed a lot of people's blood. But with each shedding of blood I felt farther away from God, more caught up in sin. How on earth could blood be used to remove sin? It was a total mystery to me, and probably part of why I wanted nothing to do with religion.

On the other hand, from the time that I had made the break with The Organization I had realized that there was something missing in my life. My every waking moment had been devoted to serving the higher power that gave the orders to members. Now I felt like I was all alone, without any backup, and no greater purpose for my life. I was just going through the motions of living, without any plan or direction. Maybe, just maybe if I started reading the Bible from page 1, I'd find something, maybe even a purpose for my life. "If you're real God, show yourself to me in this book," I said as I began reading at Genesis 1:1.

Chapter 23

The bigger picture started coming together for me when I read about Adam and Eve's sin, and how an animal had to be sacrificed to create clothing for them. The story of Cain and Abel and the sacrifice of a lamb resonated with me. That's what I'd read about before, when all I had was a New Testament to read.

As I continued reading, I began to understand what the death of Jesus on the cross meant. Before, it had just been the story of one man who got into the wrong gang's territory and his gang abandoned him and let him get killed, then never took any vengeance on his killers.

Having grown up in the culture I did, that story had no meaning to me.

Now I understood that Jesus had come to earth (our neighborhood) from heaven (his neighborhood) with the express purpose of dying for our sins, so his shed blood could cover our sins and make us ready to live with him in his neighborhood forever.

He gave himself as a sacrifice so that I wouldn't have to die.

That's the kind of person you want in your gang.

That's the kind of gang leader you ought to be willing to follow—one who is willing to give up his way in order to help you. That certainly wasn't the kind of leaders I'd found when I finally worked my way into the top ranks of The Organization I'd served all my life.

Jesus represented a Higher Power worth following, if he really was who the Bible said he was.

Finally one day, there in solitary confinement in Centinela Prison, it all came together for me in a flood of understanding that washed over me, and I realized that the hateful things I had been saying about Christianity all my life were lies.

Christianity wasn't for the weak.

Jesus wasn't weak. He was a powerful man, a powerful leader who was willing to lay aside that power if it meant he could save others in his kingdom.

If his power was real, it was the only power I wanted in my life from here on out! But what was I to do now?

I thought back to the things my friend Pete had shared with me.

Pete had continued to try to minister to me, in spite of my callous attitude toward everything he said. I'd actually gone to see him a couple of times while I was out of prison. The first time I went to the church he was pastoring, it was for all the wrong reasons. Bobby and I had pulled off a burglary in the neighborhood, and I was looking for an alibi, so I went to church.

When Pete saw me in the pew, he made a big announcement from the front. "Hey, everybody, you remember the guy I've been asking you to pray for—my home boy who's been in prison? Guess what, he's right here in church today, praise the Lord!"

I hadn't wanted to draw that much attention to myself, but it did provide a lot of witnesses to back up my alibi.

After church Pete invited me to go to a restaurant with him for lunch, and I said Sure, it would be good to catch up and talk about old times.

He got into the pickup with me, and then, right behind him came his wife Nellie and his mother-in-law Mary Garcia. Mary had sung the beautiful song "Rough Side of the Mountain" in church that day. It's one of my favorite songs. Seems the women in Pete's life were still intent on chaperoning us, making sure I didn't lead Pete back into his old ways.

I saw Pete a couple more times before I ended up back in jail, and each time we'd go out to eat together, he'd spend the whole time talking to me about Jesus and forgiveness and what God could do in my life, and I'd sit there chugging bottle after bottle of beer, nodding, and letting it go in one ear and out the other.

One time though, he got my attention.

"Mundo, you know I love you like a brother," he said, reaching across the table and putting his hand on mine.

"Yeah, sure, man. I know." I was at least sober enough to not try to make light of what he was saying.

"You know, you've been really lucky so far, *carnalito*. You're lucky to be alive."

"I know that, I know."

"You keep going the way you're going though, it ain't gonna last. One day your luck's gonna run out. You know that, don't you."

"Hey, I watch my back."

"Doesn't matter. You know it doesn't matter."

"We all gotta die sometime," I shrugged and smiled, trying to lighten the tone.

"But when that day comes, you gotta be ready. Otherwise it's over for you, and you're going straight to hell. You know that, don't you?"

"Yeah, I know that," I hung my head and looked down at the table.

Even though I'd never been religious, I had been exposed to enough theology by my grandmothers and others to realize that my life was not one that was leading me toward an eternal life of bliss.

Every time I committed a crime, I felt myself sinking farther and farther into a hole—a hell—I couldn't pull myself out of.

I'd begun to feel like the devil himself was a bird of prey on my back, that he had his talons in me, and every time I did some of his work, the talons dug in deeper. Someday, for sure, he was going to drag me kicking and screaming straight down to hell with those talons.

"Listen, Bro," he said. "There's something I want you to do for me. Will you do this one thing for me?"

"For you, anything. You know that, Fat Boy," I said, using his street name, even though in the intervening years he'd lost a lot of weight and no longer merited the moniker.

He reached into his suitcoat pocket and produced a little sheet of paper. "You see this prayer here?" The heading on the paper said "Sinner's Prayer."

"Yeah. What about it?"

"I want you to memorize it."

"Memorize it, why? That's school stuff. I don't do school stuff no more, man."

"Look, Mundo. One of these days you're going to be lying on the ground with a bullet in your back or a knife in your heart, and you're going to know it's your last day on earth. When that day comes, I want you to say this prayer, because I want to see you in heaven."

"Me—in heaven? That would be sweet but…"

"But nothing, Mundo. Read the prayer."

I looked at the paper and read it through.

Dear God in heaven, I come to you in the name of Jesus. I acknowledge to You that I am a sinner, and I am sorry for my sins and the life that I have lived; I need your forgiveness.

I believe that your only begotten Son Jesus Christ shed His precious blood on the cross at Calvary and died for my sins, and I am now willing to turn from my sin.

You said in Your Holy Word, Romans 10:9 that if we confess the Lord our God and believe in our hearts that God raised Jesus from the dead, we shall be saved.

Right now I confess Jesus as the Lord of my soul. With my heart, I believe that God raised Jesus from the dead. This very moment I accept Jesus Christ as my own personal Savior and according to His Word, right now I am saved.

Thank you Jesus for your unlimited grace which has saved me from my sins. I thank you Jesus that your grace never leads to license, but rather it always leads to repentance. Therefore Lord Jesus transform my life so that I may bring glory and honor to you alone and not to myself.

Thank you Jesus for dying for me and giving me eternal life. Amen.

I looked up at Pete. "You're telling me all I got to do is say this prayer and I can go to heaven? Like a free pass or something?"

"You got to believe it, Mundo. You got to mean it. You got to really repent of your sins, and you got to ask God to help you go straight."

I looked down at the prayer and read through it again. As I did, I felt a heaviness come over me.

Why couldn't I change my life? Why did I keep going deeper and deeper into the criminal world, even though I'd made a clean break with The Organization that I had served for so long?

I couldn't see a way out.

I couldn't see a way to live differently.

I was who I was, and I didn't know how to make a change.

But here was Pete, my best homie from years ago, the only one who'd stood by me and hadn't cut me loose after Mike got shot. He'd changed his life. He was living for God not the devil now. Maybe someday there could be hope for me.

But not today. I was in too deep.

It made me sad that I couldn't see a way to change, but maybe the day would come.

"Thanks, Pete," I said as I carefully folded the paper and stuck it into my wallet for safekeeping.

"Don't forget it," he said. "God loves you Mundo. He wants you in heaven. He wants to help you repent and get a new life."

"Yeah."

Chapter 24

I had looked at that slip of paper many times since then. I'd taken Pete's words to heart, and had memorized the prayer, so that even now in solitary confinement in Centinela State Prison, with all my physical possessions taken away from me, I had that prayer tucked away in a corner of my heart.

Over the course of a life of crime, I had watched many men die or come close to death, and over and over again, I'd heard their last words. More often than not, no matter how dedicated to the devil their life had been, their last words would be "Oh God, help me!"

Their pleas had sunk in with me.

Yes, I knew there would come a last day for me. A day when the only help I could hope for would be God's. I'd take Pete's advice and keep the prayer in my hip pocket, as a last resort, for that final day.

It all came together in my mind and heart that day in that tiny, solitary cell, and I fell to my knees crying like a baby.

Slowly the words I had memorized came out of my mouth between my sobs.

I wanted to be sure I meant each and every word,

Edmundo Ramirez

The things I had read about Jesus' shed blood and the sacrifices in the Old Testament came back to me as I prayed *"I believe that your only begotten Son Jesus Christ shed His precious blood on the cross at Calvary and died for my sins, and I am now willing to turn from my sin."*

At the end I repeated, *"Thank you Jesus for dying for me and giving me eternal life. Amen."* Then I continued to kneel there for a long time, thinking, wondering what I had just done. Would it really make any difference in my life?

I didn't feel any different.

Well, maybe the talons digging into my back had relaxed their grip a little bit. Other than that, everything seemed to be about the same.

I got slowly to my feet, wondering what had happened. Had God heard my prayer? Had he really forgiven me and removed the mountain of sins piled on my heart? There were no angels singing or bells ringing or harps playing in my cell. I was still just a poor, wretched prisoner, confined under punishing conditions.

"Did anything really happen, God?" I asked into what seemed like nothing more than thin air. "Have I really been forgiven? Will you really accept me back into your family?"

When I had read through the New Testament over and over again back in Pelican Bay, three or four years earlier, one story had resonated with me each time I came to it. The story they call The Prodigal Son. It concerns a young man who took his half of the family inheritance early, before his dad was even on his death bed, and went to a far country and squandered it.

When he was flat broke, starving on the streets, and feeding pigs for a living, he remembered that his dad gave his slaves a better deal than he was getting from the absentee land baron he was slaving for, so he decided to go home and apply for a spot on the servant staff of the ranch he'd been raised on.

But as he neared home his father was watching the roads for him and came running to him when he was still a long ways off and put his own robe on him and put the family ring on him and reclaimed him as his son.

Every time I read that story, I saw myself as that stupid kid who had wandered so far from home and squandered his life. My years from age 21 to 32 had been spent almost entirely in prison. Yes, I was that stupid kid.

But was it possible that if I would turn my face toward home, turn my face toward God, he would play the role of the father in the story who came running to his son to reclaim him for the family?

I didn't feel any robe of righteousness or warmth being wrapped around me.

I didn't see any signet ring on my finger proclaiming that I was now part of the family of God.

In fact I felt almost exactly like I had felt before I prayed the prayer.

"God, if something really happened, give me a sign. ... Please." I stood there with my head hanging, and nothing happened. "Show me something. Let me know that you heard me."

Nothing happened.

I lay down on my bunk to ponder what all this meant. Was it just wishful thinking to believe that a man like me could be forgiven and changed by some Supernatural Spirit? That there really was a Higher Power that I could turn to, a Higher Power that really cared about me as a person, not just as a soldier to carry out enforcement missions?

I really hoped so, but how could I know for sure?

I lay there for what seemed like a long time.

I may even have dozed off, but suddenly I was wide awake, my every sense tuned to the movement around me. Everything in the place was shaking! The door to my cell was rattling.

A Southern California native, I knew what to do in an earthquake, so I dived under my bunk, hoping and praying that the whole prison wouldn't collapse on top of me.

When the shaking finally stopped, I crawled back onto my bunk. "So you really do hear prayers, huh, God?" I said out loud.

Chapter 25

Don't ever be tempted to think that just because you give your life to God, everything from there on forward will be a bed of roses, and you'll immediately be empowered to overcome every temptation in your life.

It just doesn't happen that way for most people.

I know it didn't for me.

There were many tests and trials yet to face as I served out my prison term.

At first I didn't really want to change some of my old habits.

If I could score a little pot or get some wine or beer or prison hooch, I still wanted to kick back and enjoy myself.

But while I was trying to live that double life, I began having the most horrible, demonic nightmares about the devil tormenting me, tormenting little kids, all sorts of awful things happening to people, with me at the center of the action. It was like there was a spiritual battle going on in my mind, and whenever I would doze off I would be back in a horrible, dark place that I couldn't escape.

Edmundo Ramirez

I felt like I was losing my mind.

I was about ready to send a note to the prison psychologist and ask for some sort of medication to combat the paranoia I was beginning to experience.

Then one day a familiar face showed up at the door to my cell while I was in solitary. This little, stooped old man wearing a suit three sizes too large that he'd probably bought at Goodwill, came by. Sam Gaddis from Source of Light Ministry could often be seen wandering through the prison, stopping to talk to anybody who would listen, sharing tracts and Bible studies.

He stopped and looked in at me. "Need any stamps or envelopes?" he asked. "Sorry I haven't been by lately, the warden wouldn't let me come into solitary again till today."

"No, I'm good," I replied.

He peered in harder then, like he was reading something off my face. "I don't know why," he said, bending down to the push cart he always had, but God told me to give this book to you."

He handed me a small book about spiritual warfare and wearing the whole armor of God. It was based around this text from the New Testament book of Ephesians, chapter 6, verses 10-18.

Finally, be strong in the Lord and in his mighty power. Put on the full armor of God so that you can take your stand against the devil's schemes. For our struggle is not against flesh and blood, but against the rulers, against the authorities, against the powers of this dark world and against the spiritual forces of evil in the heavenly realms. Therefore put on the full armor of God, so that when the day of evil comes, you may be able to stand your ground, and after you have done everything, to stand. Stand firm then, with the belt of truth buckled around your waist, with the breastplate of righteousness in place, and with your feet fitted with the readiness that comes from the gospel of peace. In addition to all this, take up the shield of faith, with which you can extinguish all the flaming arrows of the evil one. Take the helmet of salvation and the sword of the Spirit, which is the word of God. And pray in the Spirit on all occasions with all kinds of prayers and requests. With this in mind, be alert and always keep on praying for all the saints.

(New International Version)

I was happy for some new reading material, so I started in on it right away.

Wow! This book was full of powerful insights.

As a lifetime warrior for the devil, I knew what fighting was all about—that it is natural human instinct to go right for the head when you attack someone. The author of this book understood that and explained how essential it is that a Christian wear the "helmet of salvation" to protect his head and his mind.

The book was full of practical principles for protecting oneself from Satan's attacks, quenching the devil's fiery darts with a shield dipped in the waters of baptism, walking in shoes fitted with the gospel of peace.

Gradually, as I read and studied and prayed more, the dreams subsided. And along the way I began to learn lessons about living more righteously—in a way more conducive to spiritual growth as well.

Edmundo Ramirez

Guys had ways of making wine in their cells, and they'd distribute it to their customers in small plastic bags that could be slipped under the cell door.

Three times in a row, the bag of wine I'd ordered broke on the floor before I even got a sip.

I took that as a sign and quit ordering wine, and soon I'd sworn off all intoxicants, including marijuana. I wouldn't be using any of the pages of my precious Bible to roll joints. Besides, I needed the Bible to be complete, because I was enrolled in a Bible study course that I could take through the mail in preparation for entering a life of ministry whenever I would get out.

I still had a lot of lessons to learn, though, about what it means to be a soldier for God and to fight the good fight of faith instead of the fight of the flesh that I had spent a life time honing my skills for.

Chapter 26

After a couple of years in Centinela Prison I was transferred to the California Correctional Institution in Tehachapi and placed in a cell in the maximum security portion of the prison.

I had begun to hope that my days as a warrior of the flesh were over, and that soon I would be paroled and have the chance to serve God on the outside as a spiritual warrior, using what I had learned about putting on the whole armor of God.

There at Tehachapi I met up with an old friend from the neighborhood. On the street we called him Crazy Jesse, because he would do the most insane things. I remember one time I was with him, and he saw some guys from a rival gang trying to intrude into our territory. We didn't have guns with us, but we figured they did. Anybody but Crazy Jesse would have beat a hasty retreat and gone and rounded up other soldiers to chase these guys away.

But what did Crazy Jesse do? He started throwing beer bottles at them!

And since I didn't want to look like a coward, I had to join in. Believe it or not, we managed to chase the rival gang away with nothing more than glass for weapons.

Crazy Jesse had experienced a prison conversion something like mine, and he tried to encourage me to start associating more with other Christians in the prison, but I didn't pay much attention to him. I was accustomed to running with the rough crowd, and that's where I felt at home. Some of the guys in prison who take the name Christian can be pretty creepy. A lot of inmates will take the name and play the game just to try to get on the good side of their parole board, but once they're out, they go back to their old ways. I didn't want to associate with their kind, so I continued to run with my old crowd.

But there were higher powers at work in the prison that still had their eye on me.

A week after Thanksgiving I was out in the exercise yard when I was attacked without warning by two inmates,

Before I could even react, I was on the ground, being pommeled by fists and stabbed with a prison shank.

In a flash, more inmates were involved, including a couple of my allies, and then the guards were upon us, ordering everyone to separate and lie down on the ground. My assailants didn't obey immediately, but when the second command was given, they backed off and lay down, knowing shots would soon be fired from the tower.

The officer who broke up the fight filed a report that included this description of the weapon I had been stabbed with: "The weapon was constructed from a metal rod, measuring approximately five inches in length, sharpened to a point at one end, and wrapped with cloth at the other end forming a handle." A second, similar weapon was found on the ground nearby. The men who had attacked me had come well-prepared. Their intent no doubt was to kill me for my disloyalty to The Organization. I was painfully reminded that a man like me who had once worked his way into the top echelon of that Organization would never be forgotten or forgiven if he proved disloyal.

Although I only received three stab wounds, the jacket I was wearing had more than forty holes punched in it. I was very fortunate—blessed actually—to have survived the attack with only moderate injuries.

When I was released from the infirmary, I had to spend some time in the Segregated Housing Unit (SHU), but when I was allowed back on the yard, Jesse came to me with some good advice that I was finally ready to listen to.

"You gotta quit fighting in the flesh, Bro," he said. "You gotta learn to fight in the spirit. Come on, man. Quit hanging with those guys. Join us over here in the Christian group. You'll be safer here, and learn some good stuff, too.

For the rest of my stay at Tehachapi I spent most of my time with the Christians.

Then, on April 17, 1997 I was paroled.

One week later I showed up at the Victory Outreach Church near my neighborhood, accompanied by my homie Pete.

Victory Outreach is a fellowship of more than 700 churches and ministries worldwide that was founded in 1967 by Pastor Sonny and Sister Julie Arguinzoni.

Pastor Sonny's background was in the gang-infested neighborhoods of New York (think *Westside Story*). By age 21 he was heavily into drug addiction, but was redeemed from that through Teen Challenge. While at Teen Challenge he was befriended by Nicky Cruz, whose story is told in the book and movie *The Cross and the Switchblade.*

Sonny studied at the Latin American Bible Institute in La Puente, California, where he met and married Julie Rivera. After graduation, Pastor Sonny and Sister Julie felt called to minister to recovering drug addicts. They began inviting residents of the Aliso Village housing project into their home for Bible study, and from that has grown a ministry touching the lives of hundreds of thousands of gang members and addicts all over the world.

Pastor Augie and Sister Mary Barajas began their ministry with Victory Outreach in La Puente. In 1986 they founded a church in Hollywood, and from there they moved to Glendale not far from my home.

In 1997 the congregation purchased the YMCA property in Eagle Rock. They moved into their new sanctuary just a month or two before I paroled from Tehachapi.

I attended a different church once after getting out of prison, but Pete kept insisting that I needed to come to Victory Outreach in Eagle Rock, and that's how I ended up standing in the doorway, pondering whether to go in and sit down or not. Pete had brought me to the church, but he had other things to tend to, so he left me to go into the sanctuary on my own.

And that's when I noticed that the only seat available was the one directly in front of Stretch, my homeboy that Lil T had shot five times while I stood watch eight years earlier.

It took a lot of courage and faith to take the seat in front of Stretch, but by God's grace, that's what I did.

Chapter 27

I could feel Stretch's eyes burning into my back as I stood trying to sing praises to God, the true Higher Power that had helped me turn my life around. All I could do was hope that Stretch was tuned in to that same Higher Power, not the one that had governed our lives while we were growing up.

I had heard he'd begun to attend church and was trying to get his life in order.

But could even the grace of God change a man enough that he would be able to accept and fellowship with the man who had attempted to have him assassinated?

I don't imagine either of us got much out of the sermon that Sunday. Our minds were still locked in the past.

But we both lived through it.

Stretch made a hasty exit when church was over, avoiding any contact with me.

When I told Pete I'd had to sit right in front of Stretch during the service, he just rolled his eyes and said, "Man, how did that go?"

"I don't know what he was thinking, but I know

what I was thinking—just don't stab me in the back! Let me at least look into your eyes before you kill me."

A few weeks later Pete invited me to attend a special Bible study for former gang members, where I'd get good counsel about how to put the past behind me and learn to live the Christian life. He didn't bother to tell me who else would be riding in the back seat to the meeting.

Stretch and I rode together in that back seat, all the way there and all the way back, without saying a word. Pete says he was worried that a fight was about to break out right there in the middle of the freeway, causing an accident. It was pretty intense, but we both just kept to ourselves.

The following Sunday, after church, I was standing outside in the parking lot near the children's play area when Stretch walked up. I didn't realize it, but two of his sons were playing there, and he was coming to get them.

There we were, thrown together again. Another awkward moment. I didn't look right at him, just started to make an exit.

"Mundo," he said." I need to talk to you."

That brought me up short.

I stopped and turned slowly toward him. I had a speech I'd rehearsed over and over that I had wanted to say to him, but all I could come out with was, "Yeah, I been wanting to talk to you too. I want to ask your forgiveness for what happened."

That's when this giant of a man, who had once been the devil's gladiator, but who was now partially crippled from what had gone down eight years ago, first smiled at me. "I forgive you, Bro," he said. "You know, it wasn't easy. That first time—when I saw you in church..."

"Yeah, I know man, I sat there the whole time wondering when the blade was coming out."

"I wanted to, man. Part of me really wanted to. I wanted to even the score. Let you know what it feels like to be dying."

"I don't blame you, I don't blame you a bit, man."

"But I figured I'd give it a little time. I'd heard you found Jesus, but I didn't know if it was real. Figured I'd watch. There'd be plenty of time. You weren't gonna come after a poor cripple like me, I figured."

"Yeah man, I wasn't. I totally wasn't. That was the farthest thing from my mind. I was just here to go to church, you know. Pastor Pete brought me."

"I know that now. I been watching you."

"Can you ever forgive me?"

He stuck his hands in his jeans pockets and looked down at the ground. When he looked up again, he said, "You know, Bro, there's been people. Lots of people, told me they'd be glad to come here and kill you if I gave the word."

"Yeah?"

"And there was a time I was ready to do it. But that's over now. I can see you're for real. You're really all about serving God now."

"Damn straight I am—oops, pardon my language."

He smiled. "You'll get better. It takes a while, but you'll get your vocabulary cleaned up."

He extended his hand to me then, and we clasped hands, then hugged. Two men who for years had served a higher power that could do nothing but drive us apart and lead us to do unspeakable harm to others, now united in serving the true Highest Power that would unite us in heart and spirit and in doing everything we could to help, rather than harm others.

Epilogue

In the twenty-one years since I gave my heart to the Lord there have been ups and downs. There have been times when I wondered whether I had done the right thing, whether the new Higher Power I had given my allegiance to was really still up there, watching out for me and working through me.

But I have never regretted the decision I made that day on the floor in solitary confinement at Centinela Prison.

God, the true Higher Power to whom I now swear allegiance, has seen fit to use me in many ways to help others.

When word about how Stretch and I reconciled and forgave each other spread to the church, our pastor, Augie Barajas, invited us to go with him to speak to congregations all over California. Later I was able to minister with other evangelists, sharing my testimony.

I received a great deal of help and encouragement from Victory Outreach during those early years of my Christian walk. For a time I lived in their Men's Home—a place they provide where recovering addicts and former gang members can live in a carefully-monitored environment while they develop new habits and disciplines and find employment in honorable professions.

As Stretch and I have shared our testimony of the healing power of the forgiveness and cleansing made available when Jesus gave his life on the cross, thousands of others have found salvation, forgiveness, and peace through accepting Jesus' life, death, and resurrection.

Through the kind generosity of other Christians, I was able to complete a course of study at the Latin American Bible Institute, the alma mater of Pastor Sonny and Sister Julie, preparing me for further ministry.

I've learned, since then, that even when ministering and sharing the grace of God with others, it is essential to maintain strong personal spiritual disciplines to keep your own walk with the Lord healthy.

There was a time a few years ago when I was really discouraged, almost ready to give up my Christian walk. I had been living and working down in Texas for a time. When I returned to Eagle Rock, Pastor Augie saw how I was struggling and gave me a sheet of paper that would walk me through a one-month plan for a spiritual breakthrough. By cultivating a life of prayer, study, fasting, giving, and fellowship with other Christians, it helped me refocus on good habits, getting rid of the negative influences in my life, and strengthening the strongholds.

The United Prayer International Spiritual Breakthrough worksheet for the program he suggested to me is included in the appendix, thanks to the generosity of Pastor Augie who created it.

Today I am a volunteer minister at Victory Outreach, in charge of security, and I also teach a regular anger management class. The class is court-certified by the Los Angeles County Courts, so that domestic-violence offenders are often sent to my classes as a condition of not being sent to jail.

Imagine that—the same court system that sent me to jail so often now sends offenders to my classes to let me try to help them stay out of jail!

Believe me, Bala/Bullet never could have taught a class like that. His way of handling anger was to kill or hurt somebody. But today I work with other men and women who, by nature, are like I was when my street name was Bullet. My goal is to walk them through coming to terms with God, the true Higher Power that has helped me to overcome my hurtful behaviors, and still works in me, changing me day by day to be more like the Savior I serve.

I've also started a family. My beautiful wife Maribel and I have three little girls. It's a bit late to be starting, I know. But the choices I made as a younger man put important parts of life on hold for far too long.

The devil robbed me of my youth, but now God is giving back what Satan stole from me.

My reason for sharing my story is simple.

I know there are people who feel trapped in a life of crime, violence, addiction, anger, and loss. Maybe you're one of them, and you wonder whether there really is any way out, any way to change your life.

There is.

Believe me, there is.

Edmundo Ramirez

Go back to the Sinner's Prayer on page 133. Read it through slowly and carefully, over and over till you feel you really understand it.

Ask yourself: Can I pray that prayer and mean it?

Be honest with yourself.

Don't pray it glibly, then sit back and wait for an earthquake or some other sign.

Pray it and mean it. Tell God you really do want to surrender your life to him. Then do it, and get involved with a Christian ministry that teaches love and forgiveness through Jesus. Begin your walk with God and let him lead you.

I'm not saying you'll never have struggles.

But when it comes down to the end of your life, and you're ready to go to heaven and spend eternity with Jesus, you'll know for sure that praying that prayer and really meaning it was the best thing you ever did in your life.

See you in heaven, Bro, or Sis.

APPENDIX
Mundo's Prison Records

```
RE: QHY.                              DATE:20110929 TIME:20:16:26
RESTRICTED-DO NOT USE FOR EMPLOYMENT,LICENSING OR CERTIFICATION PURPOSES
ATTN:S

*****************************************************************

DNA SAMPLE NOT VERIFIED BY FINGERPRINT HAS BEEN RECEIVED,

TYPED AND UPLOADED INTO THE CAL-DNA DATA BANK. FOR

INFO
*****************************************************************
III CALIFORNIA ONLY SOURCE RECORD
CII/F
DOB/              SEX/M  RAC/HISPANIC
HGT/5   WGT       EYE/BRO  HAI/BLK  POB/CA
NAM/01 RAMIREZ,EDMUNDO

FPC
LL
0 13 U 000 16
I 17 U 000 14
LL

FBI/6
DOB/
CDL/M
SOC/
INN/CDC-C083760
SMT/TAT R ARM; TAT CHEST; TAT L ARM
MDS/NUMEROUS TATTOOS
OCC/CARPENTRY; MAINTENANCE; WELDER
* * * *

ARR/DET/CITE:         NAM:01
19820127  CAPD LOS ANGELES

CNT:01    #1716596-R 6477546
  211 PC-ROBBERY                                      TOC:F
- - - -
COURT:                NAM:01
19820621  CASC LOS ANGELES CENTRAL

CNT:01    #A375639
  211 PC-ROBBERY                                      TOC:F
  DISPO:DISMISSED/FOJ/INSUFFICIENT EVIDENCE
* * * *

ARR/DET/CITE:         NAM:01
19830628  CAPD LOS ANGELES

CNT:01    #1716596R-7172294
  11378.5 HS-POSSESS PHENCYCLIDINE/ETC FOR SALE       TOC:F
19830630
  DISPO:PROS REL-DET ONLY/LACK OF PROB CAUS/EVID
* * * *

ARR/DET/CITE:         NAM:01
19830912  CAPD LOS ANGELES

CNT:01    #1716596R-7269767
  187 PC-MURDER                                       TOC:F
* * * *
```

Page 1 of 4

157

Edmundo Ramirez

```
CUSTODY:CDC              NAM:01
19810406  CASD CORR CHINO

CNT:01     #C83760
  192.2 PC-INVOLUNTARY MANSLAUGHTER                       TOC:F
  -USED FIREARM
  SEN FROM: LOS ANGELES CO   CRT #A-394492
  SEN: 5 YEARS PRISON

19861011
 DISPO:PAROLED
   RECVD BY:CAPA ALAMEDA CO
 * * * *


ARR/DET/CITE:            NAM:01
19850312  CASD CORR SOLEDAD

CNT:01     #C-83760
  -IN PRISON ARR
  4501 PC-ASSAULT BY PRISONER                             TOC:F
19850326
 DISPO:PROS REJECT/VICTIM UNAVAIL/DECLINE PROS
 * * * *

CUSTODY:CDC              NAM:01
19861224  CASD CORR CHINO

CNT:01     #C83760
  VIOLATION OF PAROLE                                     TOC:N
  -TO FINISH TERM
 * * * *


ARR/DET/CITE:            NAM:01
19870829  CAPD LOS ANGELES

CNT:01     #1716596R-9261606
  12021(A) PC-FELON/ADDICT/ETC POSSESS FIREARM            TOC:F
19870916
 DISPO:PROS REL-DET ONLY/LACK OF PROB CAUS/EVID
 * * * *


CUSTODY:CDC              NAM:01
19871007  CASD CORR CHINO CENTRAL

CNT:01     #C83760
  VIOLATION OF PAROLE                                     TOC:N
  -TO FINISH TERM
 * * * *


ARR/DET/CITE:            NAM:01  DOB:19610716
19890402  CAPD LOS ANGELES

CNT:01     #1716596R 1314980
  -ATTEMPTED
  187(A) PC-MURDER                                        TOC:F
 - - - -
COURT:                   NAM:01
19891003  CASC LOS ANGELES CENTRAL

CNT:01     #A986157
  -ATTEMPTED
  211 PC-ROBBERY                                          TOC:F
 DISPO:DISMISSED/FURTHERANCE OF JUSTICE
```

```
CNT:02
  245(A)(1) PC-FORCE/ADW NOT FIREARM:GBI LIKELY          TOC:F
*DISPO:CONVICTED
   CONV STATUS:FELONY
   SEN: 4 YEARS PRISON
  * * * *


CUSTODY:CDC              NAM:01
19891017  CASD CORRECTIONS

CNT:01     #C83760
  245(A)(1) PC-FORCE/ADW NOT FIREARM:GBI LIKELY          TOC:F
   SEN FROM: LOS ANGELES CO  CRT #A986157
   SEN: 4 YEARS PRISON
  * * * *


ARR/DET/CITE:           NAM:01
19891115  CASD CORR CHINO

CNT:01     #C83760
  -IN PRISON ARR
  4501 PC-ASSAULT BY PRISONER                           TOC:F
19900109
 DISPO:PROS REJECT/REASON UNKNOWN


CNT:02
  -IN PRISON ARR
  4502 PC-PRISONER POSSESS WEAPON                       TOC:F
19900109
 DISPO:PROS REJECT/REASON UNKNOWN
  * * * *


ARR/DET/CITE:           NAM:01
19910515  CASD CORR PELICAN BAY

CNT:01     #C83760
  -IN PRISON ARR
  4502 PC-PRISONER POSSESS WEAPON                       TOC:F
19920120
 DISPO:PROS REJ-LACK OF SUFFICIENT EVIDENCE


CNT:02
  -IN PRISON ARR
  653F PC-SOLICIT SPECIFIED CRIMINAL ACTS               TOC:F
  * * * *


ARR/DET/CITE:           NAM:01  DOB:19610716
19930514  CAPD AZUSA

CNT:01     #933794-3782003
  459 PC-BURGLARY                                       TOC:F
  - - - -
COURT:                  NAM:01
19930929  CASC LOS ANGELES POMONA

CNT:01     #KA017628
  459 PC-BURGLARY:FIRST DEGREE                          TOC:F
  -W/PR FEL CONV
*DISPO:CONVICTED
   CONV STATUS:FELONY
   SEN: 7 YEARS PRISON, RESTN
  * * * *


CUSTODY:CDC              NAM:01
```

Edmundo Ramirez

```
19931021  CASD CORRECTIONS

CNT:01    #C83760
  459 PC-BURGLARY:FIRST DEGREE                    TOC:F

CNT:02
  667(A) PC-PRIOR FELONY CONVICTION               TOC:N
  SEN FROM:LOS ANGELES CO
  SEN: 7 YEARS PRISON
  COM: CTN KA017628
  COM: CCN-6116D172941
    *    *    *    END OF MESSAGE    *    *    *
```

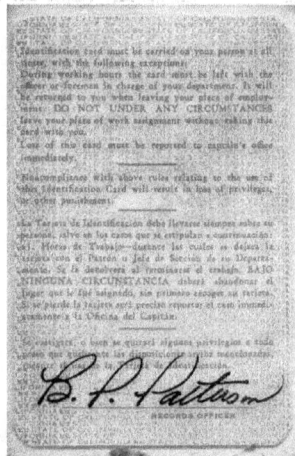

CALIFORNIA INSTITUTION FOR MEN COMPLEX

RECEPTION CENTER CENTRAL

DATE: 15 November 1989
INCIDENT LOG NO: 0459

TO: , Sergeant (A)
Second Watch Housing Sergeant
Reception Center Central

FROM: , Correctional Officer
Second Watch Cypress Hall Officer
Reception Center Central

SUBJECT: <u>INCIDENT REPORT - STABBING ASSAULT ON AN INMATE IN CYPRESS
HALL.</u>

At approximately 1505 hours this date, I was on the Third Tier,
Eastside of CYPRESS HALL, preparing to release
        from RTQ Cell 77, to escort him for a bed move to Palm
Hall. I heard the sounds of fighting, and immediately proceeded
to Cell 77 where I observed RAMIREZ, Edmundo C-83760 and
                      inside Cell 77, fighting. I activated my
personal alarm, and notified my cover officer that there was a
fight in progress in Cell 77.   I ordered the inmates to stop
fighting. I observed what appeared to be an inmate-made weapon
in the right hand of inmate RAMIREZ.   was holding
RAMIREZ' right wrist, in an apparent attempt to keep RAMIREZ from
stabbing him with the weapon. I continued to order the inmates
to stop fighting. I observed RAMIREZ move to the commode in the
cell and flush the weapon. Responding staff arrived, the cell
was entered, both inmates placed in restraints, and escorted out
of the unit.

On your instructions, I collected and searched the property of
both inmates. I have also prepared CDC-115 Rules Violation
Reports charging them both with violation of CCR Section
DR-3005(C) Force and Violence, for RAMIREZ, the specific act of
committing a stabbing assault on another inmate; for
the specific act of being involved in a stabbing assault on an
inmate.

                    l D. ... 3, Correctional Officer
                    Second Watch Cypress Hall Officer
                    Reception Center Central

161

Edmundo Ramirez

State of California

M E M O R A N D U M

Date: April 12, 1991

To: . . a A a Captain
         Security & Investigations Unit

From: **Pelican Bay State Prison**
       P.O. Box 7000, Crescent City, CA. 95531-7000

Subject: **GANG STATUS OF EDMUNDO RAMIREZ C83760 ("BULLET")**

On 12 April, 1991, I reviewed the Central File of inmate Edmundo RAMIREZ
C83760 (AKAs "Bullet"/ "Bala"/ "Mundo" from Cypress Avenues) for the purpose of updating his status with the Mexican Mafia prison gang. Currently
there is sufficient information to consider him as an associate of the
EME. The following documentation supports this opinion:

  (1) Conf. Memo 8-01-90 in which a confidential informant identified
      RAMIREZ as an associate of the EME, and a member of the Avenues
      street gang.   (Confidential Informant)

  (2) CDC 128B 4-12-91: Names and addresses of EME members discovered
      in RAMIREZ's property during a cell search.

  (3) Conf. Memo 1-29-90 in which a confidential informant identified
      RAMIREZ as an EME associate who stabbed ▇▇▇▇▇▇▇▇▇▇ for the
      EME on 11-15-89.   (Confidential Informant)

  (4) Conf. Memo 3-19-90 in which a letter discussing AB and EME members
      and associates identifies subject among a group of EME members at
      L.A. County Jail. Because neither the author nor recipient were
      validated EME members, this can only be used as supporting informa-
      tion, rather than source documentation. (Correspondence)

In addition to being an associate of the EME, there is sufficient document
ation to consider RAMIREZ as a member of the Cypress Avenues street gang.
This is based upon the following:

  (1) **Tattoos** depicting "Ave's Cyp's" for Cypress Avenues. See a photocopy
      attached to this report.   (Tattoo)

  (2) Conf. ... 7-. ..), in which a confidential informant identified him
      as a member of the Avenues. (Confidential Informant)

  (3) F . 3-)- 1, in which subject, while in the company of other Avenues
      street gang members, accidentally shot one of his fellow gang mem-
      bers while firing his weapon randomly. RAMIREZ was under the influ-
      ence of PCP and alcohol at the time. (Commitment Offense)

GANG STAUS OF RAMIREZ C83760
April 12, 1991
Page 2

(4) Staff Evaluation 4-30-84 in which subject admitted to being a member
of the Avenues since about 1977.   (Self-Admission)

(5) Conf. Memo 8-1-90, in which a confidential informant identified him
as "Bullet" from Avenues. (Confidential Informant)

I interviewed RAMIREZ on this date regarding the information being used to
identify his gang status. RAMIREZ denies association with the EME and that
he has the aliases of "Vala" or "Bullet". RAMIREZ also denies any current
affiliation with the Avenues street gang since his accidental shooting of
his "homeboy". In regards to the stabbing of ███████ subject stated that
it was a personal problem and not gang-related.

Subject, however, should be considered as an associate of the EME, and a
member of the Cypress Avenues.

Correctional Sergeant
Gang Investigator (A)

Edmundo Ramirez

DEPARTMENT OF CORRECTIONS   STATE OF CALIFORNIA

ORDER AND HEARING FOR PLACEMENT IN SEGREGATED HOUSING

An inmate is entitled to a written decision including references to the evidence relied upon and the reasons for such confinement. A copy of the completed form must be given to the inmate, a copy placed in the central file, and a copy retained in a central location at the institution.

Prior to initial placement, or within 48 hours of such placement, an inmate is entitled to written notice of the reasons for placement in sufficient detail to enable the inmate to prepare a response or defense.

PART I NOTICE OF REASONS FOR PLACEMENT IN ADMINISTRATIVE SEGREGATION

NAME	NUMBER	INSTITUTION
RAMIREZ	C 83760	PBSP SHU

A determination has been made to place you in segregated housing. The reasons for such placement are:

You are being placed in Administrative Segregation pending CSR endorsement of the ICC Action of 4/25/1991 recommending PBSP SHU Indeterminate Status due to your Association with the Mexican Mafia Prison Gang (EME), upon the completion of you SHU Term with a MERD of 5/16/1991. You are deemed a threat to the safety of others and to the Security of the Institution, based on your continued association with the EME Prison Gang, that engages in criminal activities.

                                                            , C/LE. PBSP SHU

INMATE SIGNATURE		
		☐ Refused to Sign
☑ Copy Given to Inmate	EMPLOYEE	DATE 5-16-91

Representation by counsel-substitute is required when it is determined that the inmate is illiterate or that the complexity of the issues makes it unlikely that he/she can collect and present the evidence necessary for an adequate comprehension of the case. This determination must be made at the time of initial placement or within 48 hours of such placement. (Complete both A and B below.)

PART II COUNSEL-SUBSTITUTE

A. STAFF ASSISTANT (Assigned if inmate is illiterate or issues complex.)

☐ Not Assigned   ☐ Inmate Not Illiterate

☐ Inmate Declines   ☐ Issues Not Complex

☐ Assigned   (Name) _____

Other Reasons or Comments:

B. INVESTIGATING EMPLOYEE (Assigned when inmate is not illiterate and issues are not complex but assistance is necessary to enable inmate to collect and present evidence necessary for an adequate comprehension of the case.)

☐ Not Assigned   ☐ Inmate Declines

                                         ☐ Inmate Able to Collect and Present Evidence

☐ Assigned   (Name) _____

Other Reasons and Comments:

CDC 114-D (1-79)   *(See Reverse Side)*

804 TO RECORDS AND NEW TRACK ON _____ BY _____

STATE OF CALIFORNIA
RULES VIOLATION REPORT
1192
DEPARTMENT OF CORRECTIONS

CDC NUMBER	INMATE'S NAME		RELEASE/BOARD DATE	INST.	HOUSING NO	LOG NO. NKPR-D-
C-83760	RAMIREZ	(M)		N.K.S.P.	FDB6 119L	93-12-0002
VIOLATED RULE NO(S)	SPECIFIC ACTS			LOCATION	DATE	TIME
CCR §3005(c) FORCE & VIOLENCE	PHYSICAL ALTERCATION			AD/SEG YARD	12-3-93	1525

CIRCUMSTANCES

On 12-3-93 at approximately 1525 hours, I was preparing to escort the inmates back to their cells from the Administrative Segregation yard #3 when suddenly Inmate RAMIREZ, C-83760, FDB6-119L charged at Inmate ___, ___, ___. RAMIREZ began striking ___ with clenched fists about the head and upper body. ___ attempted to defend himself by fighting back. I ordered both inmates to stop fighting and for all the inmates on the yard to lay down on the ground. All inmates complied with the exception of RAMIREZ and ___ who continued to fight. Both RAMIREZ and ___ ignored repeated orders to stop fighting and stopped only after tower #8 fired a warning shot from his state issued Ruger Mini-14 rifle. Both inmates were medically evaluated and treated for minor abrasions and housed back in their assigned cells without further incident. Inmate RAMIREZ is aware of this report.

REPORTING EMPLOYEE	DATE	ASSIGNMENT	RDO S
___, Correctional Officer	12-3-93	FDB6 AD/SEG S&E	T/W
REVIEWING SUPERVISOR'S SIGNATURE ___ SGT.	12-3-93		

HEARING

Inmate RAMIREZ stated he was in good health, sound state of mind, acknowledged receipt of all reports to be used as evidence and was ready to proceed with the hearing. All reports were issued more than 24 hours prior to the hearing. Witnesses WERE NOT requested. The charges were read to Inmate RAMIREZ and he pled GUILTY. INMATE'S STATEMENT: No statement. An I.E. was assigned.
FINDINGS: Inmate RAMIREZ was found GUILTY of violating CCR §3005(c), SPECIFIC ACT: Physical Altercation. The evidence presented at the hearing SUBSTANTIATES the charge. The evidence included: Reporting employee's written report. Inmate's own admission of guilt.
DISPOSITION: GUILTY. Assessed 90 days loss of behavior credits for Division "D" offense.

Inmate RAMIREZ was advised of his rights and the procedure to appeal this action and that he would receive a copy within five days of CDO audit.

ACTION BY (TYPED NAME)	SIGNATURE	DATE	TIME
L. Roll - Lieutenant		12-12-93	0910 Hrs

165

Edmundo Ramirez

STATE OF CALIFORNIA

DEPARTMENT OF CORRECTIONS

RULES VIOLATION REPORT

CDC NUMBER	INMATE'S NAME		RELEASE/BOARD DATE	INST.	HOUSING NO.	LOG NO.
C-83760	RAMIREZ		RRD:	CENTINELA	C1-123U	FC-94-02-00
VIOLATED RULE NO(S)		SPECIFIC ACTS RESISTING STAFF DURING A		LOCATION	DATE	TIME
CCR § 3005 (C)		PHYSICAL ALTERCATION WITH OTHER INMATES	DINING HALL	02-10-94	0800 HOURS

CIRCUMSTANCES

On February 10, 1994 at approximately 0800 hours, in Facility "C" Dining Hall, I observed Inmate
, in a fighting stance with both hands clenched. Inmate .
struck Inmate Ramirez, C-83760, FCB1-123U, with a right clenched fist on the left side of his
face. I ordered Inmate Ramirez down into the prone position in which he refused. As I placed
my hands on his shoulders to pull Inmate Ramirez down from behind, we twisted and Inmate Ramirez
landed on the right inside part of myknee. I then placed mechanical restraints(handcuff) on
Inmate Ramirez and escorted him to the Medical Technical Assistant.

(Typed Name and Signature)		DATE	ASSIGNMENT	RDO'S
CORRECTIONAL OFFICER		02-10-94		M-T

REVIEWING SUPERVISOR'S SIGNATURE		DATE	☐ INMATE SEGREGATED PENDING HEARING		
CORRECTION SGT.		02-10-94	DATE 02-10-94	LOC. A5-122L	

CLASSIFIED	OFFENSE DIVISION	DATE	CLASSIFIED BY (Typed Name and Signature)	HEARING REFERRED TO			
☐ ADMINISTRATIVE			▶	☐ HO	☐ SHO	☐ SC	☐ FC
☑ SERIOUS							

COPIES GIVEN INMATE BEFORE HEARING				
☑ CDC 115	BY: (STAFF'S SIGNATURE)	DATE	TIME	TITLE OF SUPPLEMENT
115 A	▶	2-1-94	1320	7219
☑ INCIDENT REPORT LOG NUMBER: 3C-94-02-0008	BY: (STAFF'S SIGNATURE) ▶	DATE 3-2-94	TIME 1000 (m)	BY: (STAFF'S SIGNATURE) ▶	DATE	TIME 2.3

HEARING

REFERRED TO ☐ CLASSIFICATION ☐ BPT/NAEA				
ACTION BY: (TYPED NAME)		SIGNATURE ▶	DATE	TIME
REVIEWED BY: (SIGNATURE) ▶	DATE	CHIEF DISCIPLINARY OFFICER'S SIGNATURE ▶	DATE	
☐ COPY OF CDC 115 GIVEN INMATE AFTER HEARING	BY: (STAFF'S SIGNATURE) ▶		DATE	TIME

The Spiritual Breakthrough Worksheet

United Prayer International Spiritual Breakthrough	DAY	1	2	3	4	5	6	7	8	9	10	11	12	13	14	15	16	17	18	19	20	21	22	23	24	25	26	27	28	29	30	31
A - Prayer																																	
B - God's Word																																	
C - Fasting																																	
D - Giving																																	
E - Attend Church																																	
Good Habits:																																	
1)																																	
2)																																	
3)																																	
Bad Habits:																																	
1)																																	
2)																																	
3)																																	
Strongholds:																																	
1)																																	
2)																																	
3)																																	

Abide in the Lord   A - Phillipians 4:6 / James 5:16   C - Isaiah 58:6 / Matthew 17:21   E - Heb. 10:25 / Act. 2:46-47

John 15:7   B - Matthew 4:4 / Joshua 1:8   D - Matthew 6:19-21 / 1Tim. 6:10

The spiritual breakthrough worksheet that Pastor Augie shared to encourage me in my walk with the Lord. Before adopting these disciplines, I had become discouraged and begun to wonder whether God was still working in my life.

By using this checklist to guide me in my daily walk, I was revived and once again able to walk confidently and share my faith.

Prison Days

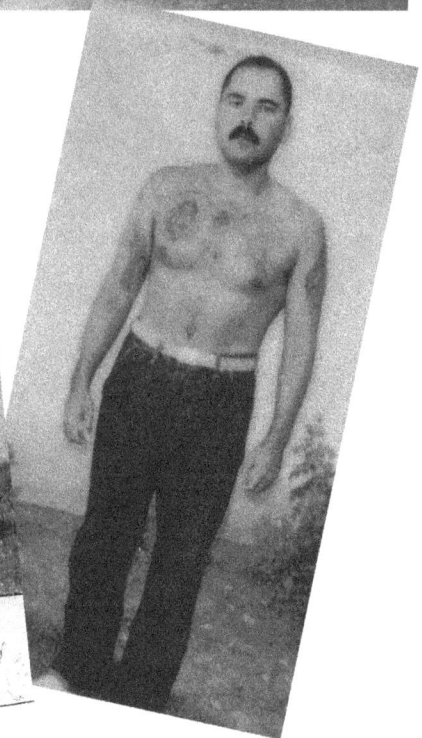

Visiting my nephew's grave shortly after release from prison in 1997. David Anthony Valenzuela, "Little Bullet," was shot and killed in my neighborhood while walking home in 1996.

Pete and Nellie Reese, my roll dog and his wife, Pastor to the Homies.

A poster featuring Stretch from a recent church meeting.

With Stretch recently. He's still a lot taller than I am.

FROM THE WRITER

In telling Mundo's story I have attempted to faithfully recreate the world he lived in, and to portray the man he was before he was remade by God. If you were to meet Mundo today, if you didn't see his tattoos, you would never guess that this man was once a hardened criminal who remembered his time in California's most violent prison, Folsom, with the nostalgia of a college grad looking back on his frat house days.

The Mundo I have come to know and love while writing his story is a kind, soft-spoken, faithful father of three darling little girls. To try to picture him looking through steely eyes at a trembling victim whose life he is about to take defies imagination. His life, more than almost any I have heard of, gives credence to the idea that there is a God of love who longs to come into the life of even the most hardened sinner and remake him or her in the image of Jesus.

Ken Wade
April, 2015

Edmundo Ramirez

Other books by Ken Wade
  Secrets of the New Age
  Savage Future
  There's Always Hope
  The Orion Conspiracy
  Back on Track
  Jesus for a New Millennium
  The Joy of Jesus
  Del Delker
  Journey to Moriah
  Paul: A Spiritual Journey
  Really Living-1
  Really Living-2
  Journey Through the Bible: Genesis to Job
  Journey Through the Bible: Psalms to Malachi
  Journey Through the Bible: Matthew to Revelation
  Secret Corners

Bound by Blood

Edmundo Ramirez

www.ingramcontent.com/pod-product-compliance
Lightning Source LLC
Chambersburg PA
CBHW070800100426
42742CB00012B/2201